AF418030

The Fruit that lasts

The Fruit that lasts

For the people

who like to learn

and unite for the mission

Normand THOMAS

Other books by the author:
A path to conversion
Daily path to conversion
Let's reveal God
Refusing sin
Let's love God
Let's be Loved
... for Love
The heart's mission
Watch with faith
The Shepherd's Mission

Normand Thomas
1964 –

Email: jesuseigneur@gmail.com

English translation from French :
Le Fruit qui demeure

Introduction

The Holy Spirit passes in hearts and between people. The Church is moving when its members become fervent. The Church is growing and the Holy Spirit is helping to multiply its members. John writes in his first letter:

"Children, let us love not in word or speech but in deed and truth." *1 John, chapter 3, verse 18*

What seems most difficult in the mission is to mention what is needed at the appropriate time or for the appropriate activity, meeting. It is about being in the best disposition of ourselves and knowing the one we're talking about, in truth. Are we really talking about God?

Even though sometimes the deeds and words are not always in accord with the Gospels, since we are not perfect, let's continue to improve our relationship with people. And if we succeed, may we remember that we have done only what we could.

+ Please pray for me

Respecting our limit

Pathway 67

Balance

> Behold, this too is vanity. Here is a man who has laboured with wisdom and knowledge and skill, and to another, who has not laboured over it, he must leave his property. This also is vanity and a great misfortune.
>
> For what profit comes to a man from all the toil and anxiety of heart with which he has laboured under the sun? *Ecclesiastes, chapter 2, verses 1 and 21 to 22*

We are invited to invest ourselves with balance. Some people try to achieve everything and they are so engaged in all kinds of activities that they don't realize that they are harming their health ... even sometimes the health of others.

What are our priorities? Can we offer more of our services to the Church, for the world? Do we carry out activities that will bring us closer to a relationship with Jesus and help others to know him? Or are we just looking to put on a show, to look good, occupied?

It's always easier to participate in the life of the Church than to leave the work to one or two people. It's also necessary that those who work in the Church leave some space for others.

Talents

Let's invest in something that resembles us, brings us together and reflects our talents, supported by the teaching of the Church. It may seem simple, but it's good to think about it properly to fit and meet our talents.

Each person has his own charisms. It's also recommended to ask the Holy Spirit what would be best for us to achieve.

There are always people in the Church who hold on despite the adversity of everything that keeps the world away from churches. They hold on and that keeps the Church fruitful. They receive courage and tenacity from Our Lord. Glory be to Jesus!

Paul tells us:

"Think of what is above, not of what is on earth." *Colossians, chapter 3, verse 2*

May all that we do for the people be inspired by the realities from above. The realities of the earth are good and pleasant, like picking strawberries, but the realities of heaven are superior to them, like the fruit of charity toward people.

Seeds

Jesus invites us to think:

"Friend, who appointed me as your judge and arbitrator?" *Luke, chapter 12, verse 14*

Jesus is not a judge as we may think. He doesn't judge us as we often do. He lets us judge of what we achieve. He lets us decide if we want to share the goods of the kingdom of God that we carry within us. He even questions us. He wonders why we perceive him as a judge, in the sense of a referee.

Let's ask Jesus to help recognize in us what we can share of our spiritual life, so that his Heart overflows on people and between hearts.

As the fields and the valleys are full of fruits and vegetables that feed us, all our actions and words are full of divine and beneficial seeds for those around us.

Let's gather the fruits of paradise and fill our baskets with hope, faith, charity and also prudence, temperance, strength and justice; the strength and righteousness that are from the Love of God, and offer them to all, so that they too may discover the beauty and wonder of the divine fields of God.

Without tiring

"They that hope in the Lord will renew their strength, they will soar as with eagles' wings; they will run and not grow weary, walk and not grow faint." *Isaiah, chapter 40, verse 31*

We must constantly remind ourselves that we are missionaries of faith, but faith is transmitted by Jesus:

"He who watches for her [wisdom] at dawn shall not be disappointed, for he shall find her sitting by his gate." *Wisdom, chapter 6, verse 14*

There's no need to seek wisdom, let's welcome it, in us. To receive it requires no effort, it will not tire us out. This is God's key.

To place our hope, to place our trust in the Lord, means to let him be God and allow him to act for all. It's not easy to achieve when we're invited to become missionaries of faith in the world and leave it to Jesus to join people. Let's face it, usually we like to do everything ourselves.

It's like we're grocery shopping, but we can't touch the food we need. Someone else will put it in our basket.

With God, the provision basket of faith is full and overflowing. We've only to develop the intention to receive the fruits. We only need to adjust ourselves to him, to adore the Word of God and the Eucharist and to be willing to receive everything from God.

May Jesus have all the space in us to realize salvation in our hearts. He knows what is in each person's heart. The more we leave space to Jesus, the more he can work in his human family. May he garnish our basket of wonderful and nourishing fruits of the sky to offer them to the hungriest and most lacking in faith. Let's place our trust in Jesus, because Jesus alone really knows the heart and the needs of his children.

However, in life, for our body, it's desirable and normal to do what is necessary to live. We have to pick good food to share and eat.

We get tired

Let's give back the worries of the mission that we carry in the hands of the master. Jesus, himself, invites us to give him the weight we carry. He wants us to rest:

> Come to me, all you who labour and are burdened, and I will give you rest. Take my yoke upon you and learn from me, for I am meek and humble of heart; and you will find rest for your selves. For my yoke is easy, and my burden light. *Matthew, chapter 11, verses 28 to 30*

In all hearts, it is possible to hear this message from Jesus: "Come to me." Evangelization is successful when a person is freely led to Jesus. We have no reason to force it and, by the very fact, to tire ourselves for nothing.

Strangely, the person who wants to force other people to convert will lose energy and it may distort the progress of his faith. It's like wanting to run after a bird. The bird is free to fly. Or to push on a turtle for it to go faster. The turtle is already doing what it should and what it can. It's free to be humble in its approach. That's what makes it beautiful. This is what makes the bird and turtle unique.

It is in our heart to welcome others and to inform them well while leaving them the freedom to approach Jesus at their own pace. We present them the fruits, but it's up to them to choose and eat them, for a day to serve in turn, when ready.

The person who doesn't want to welcome him will get tired, then exhaust in fighting God's call. Even if the person is free thanks to God, he shuts off because of his refusal. The call of God remains present though.

Some don't know how to receive him. But it's so simple. They only need to ask Jesus to enter into their lives, with the will to put their lives in his hands. This can be done now from heart to Heart.

Let's ask Jesus to touch them. He will. And even if Jesus passed in them, it may take time for us to see his presence. We only need to be attentive to the good, beautiful, true and real in them. He's there for sure.

The Holy Spirit wants to go through our hearts to touch people's lives. This is our mission, to receive the Spirit. But it is he who evangelizes. Evangelization is when the Spirit is allowed to go through us, to touch the hearts of people.

The Holy Spirit can also pass into the hearts without us participating. He is the master of hearts. It all depends on the opening of each person's heart. This is where the realization of evangelization is played out. If we accept the presence of the Lord in our life, we will receive what's necessary to grow in faith and offer it.

Happy are the people who answer the call of God and make of him the Lord of their lives.

Give it up to give

In this next text, we can imagine people represented by trees, whistling in the air because they don't want to leave what characterizes them, their wealth and their talents to serve the neighbour.

Yotam is stationed on the summit of Mount Garizim and he shouts with all his strength:

> When this was reported to him, Jotham went to the top of Mount

Gerizim, and standing there, cried out to them in a loud voice: "Hear me, citizens of Shechem, that God may then hear you! Once the trees went to anoint a king over themselves. So they said to the olive tree, 'Reign over us.' But the olive tree answered them, 'Must I give up my rich oil, whereby men and gods are honored, and go to wave over the trees?' Then the trees said to the fig tree, 'Come; you reign over us!' But the fig tree answered them, 'Must I give up my sweetness and my good fruit, and go to wave over the trees?' Then the trees said to the vine, 'Come you, and reign over us.' But the vine answered them, 'Must I give up my wine that cheers gods and men, and go to wave over the trees?'" *Judges, chapter 9, verses 7 to 13*

Yotam tells a story to people so that they understand. He thus checks their honesty. Many trees are asked if they want to rule the forest. But the olive tree is afraid of losing its oil which serves man and God. The fig tree fears to give up the sweetness and the flavour of its fruits. The vine doesn't want to give up its wine, which rejoices humans and God.

Yet all these creatures of God lose nothing in offering what they have received from him. They will lose everything anyway, since their fruits will fall to the ground and they will no longer serve humans.

It would be better to offer them for the good of others. Picking doesn't change their nature. They will give fruit again, sometimes more abundant, year after year.

Of all that the person has in him, it's similar. The fruits of the Spirit and the aroma of the person don't change, even if he becomes responsible for an activity in the local church. Nothing is lost. On the contrary, he gains experience to improve the quality of his faith. Then, it offers fruits in abundance, received from the Spirit, to feed humans. He lets himself be picked.

But the trees do not want the responsibility to look after the forest. They say to the bush of thorns:

"Come; you reign over us!" *Judges, chapter 9, verse 14*

They turn to the bush. The thorn bush understood that the trees are too proud. He challenges them:

"If you wish to anoint me king over you in good faith, come and take refuge in my shadow. Otherwise, let fire come from the buckthorn and devour the cedars of Lebanon" *Judges, chapter 9, verse 15*

... otherwise, you are not sincere.

The bush is the smallest of all in this story, but we understand that he knows how to observe and see reality. He looks up, but the other trees can't see what's happening down there.

According to this story, what gift of God are we willing to share to serve our neighbour? What are we willing to share to become workers in the service of the Lord?

Everything we own can be passed on for the good of the people. If we keep our talents, our riches only for ourselves, we lose our abilities and time. All we receive from God is to share wisely with other people. Justice, fraternal charity begins here. The sharing of what we have and often our surplus is to be attentive to the ones in need.

For fruit trees, it doesn't require an extra effort to be generous. They already have something to offer and it comes from God. We also receive everything from the Lord.

The good wine

Jesus keeps knocking at the door of our heart, to invite us to enter into the dance and joy of the children of God, and he invites us to work with him. When we accept, the harvest becomes abundant and the workers of the world come to gather what they need. We allow others to discover what they are looking for ... happiness in God.

Let's ask the master of the seed to send labourers for sowing. Let's ask the master of the mission to send workers to his mission. Let's ask the master of evangelization to send people to evangelize. Let's ask the Lord of the harvest to send out labourers for the harvest. Jesus needs people who feed on the Word and the Eucharist, who share their faith and who are happy christians among the people, his great family.

The testimony of christians becomes the good wine that pleases people's hearts. People will want to find out from where is coming the source they drink from. One day, they will perceive that they drink to the Spirit that was sent to us by Christ.

We are therefore invited to share our internal resources:

"The community of believers was of one heart and mind, and no one claimed that any of his possessions was his own, but they had everything in common." *Acts, chapter 4, verse 32*

In the Church and especially in a community, the difference between people is a privilege. Each person has his place, keeps his identity and his own charisms. Each one share what he is and what he has different from others. Harmony is realized by these differences, together.

Profound sadness for a community if everyone wants to be similar. It's more important to know ourselves better, to better discover who we really are than to begin to convey a false image of ourselves. We need everyone and their differences in the Church to reach people's hearts. And also, let's welcome our own personal difference. That's what gives colour to the community.

The authenticity of people is a treasure trove of truth and reality in a community. In this way we can return to what Paul shares with us: "The community of believers was of one heart and mind, and no one claimed that any of his possessions was his own, but they had everything in common."

When we share our different strengths, our different gifts and charisms, our different projects of evangelization and put them in common, our different good attitudes and colours together, we develop a community that marvels at every moment.

There's nothing more damaging to a community than people seeking to be identical to others. We're not talking here about the community's own mission, but about the colour that each of its members brings.

What is similar for all is that we receive all of this from God, through prayer, and we share it with a charitable heart. The Passover light and the Mercy of the Trinity circulate in a community like this.

We're not perfect, but to become authentic people living in the realm of Jesus is a blessing for all, both in the Church and in the world.

As Jesus says:

"If I tell you about earthly things and you do not believe, how will you believe if I tell you about heavenly things?" *John, chapter 3, verse 12*

Being realistic about what is going on in the world teaches us at the same time to be realistic in understanding the realities of heaven.

Being authentic with ourselves allows us to discover all the riches and transmit all that God has already given us. We're called to a great mission where God is the one who does everything for the world. It's a privilege to be called, to be attentive and invited to participate. It is a privilege. It reaches the hearts of people and it touches us to see their smiles, fuelled by the heart, growing on their faces.

We pray, we celebrate Mass, we worship the Lord in the Eucharist and in his Word alike, and we become authentic people, of course.

Mutual aid

If there are people who can help in one area or another, mechanics, caretaking, fraternal listening, helping one of the members in one of his needs, according to their talents, the help will be appreciated and they will receive a hundredfold from the Lord.

It would be easier to have about twenty people who offer their services than just a few who do everything. That doesn't prevent that the generosity is at hand when there is an important work to accomplish in the churches. Often people give themselves without counting in big events. Many people offer their services discreetly, without anyone being aware. All these people are generous.

To leave our task, when there's no one to assume it and to take over, for example, is to take risks, it's mortgaging the immediate future of the responsibilities and the activities of evangelization in the church.

Let's think of other people who could share our tasks, while we still have the capacity to do them. In this way, if something happens to us, a loss of health, an accident or a new job, a new opportunity for example, we know that the mission will continue. In addition, it allows others to walk in faith as they offer their services.

The First Leader

For all those who have carried out projects or participated in church activities, it is appreciated. But let's remember that we all work with Jesus. We don't do a job for a parish official, for the priest, for the bishop, for the pope, but together with Jesus for his Church, and for her to continue her mission of salvation so much needed in and for the world.

We all participate in the future of the Church and for the next generations, right now. Thus it's more fitting that it be Jesus who thanks us. May Jesus thank those who work in the Church, and say something to our hearts. Let's listen to him.

Jesus, with the Father and the Holy Spirit, is the reason why we are Church. He's the First Leader. Jesus is the reason we come and work together in prayer, sharing, helping one another. May Jesus fill us with his presence and his Love.

Sometimes we get the impression that we can't do something or that we can't read, for example, because we fear that people will judge us, that they will think us above everyone. But we can leave the "what will they say" and work with Jesus. It is Jesus who invites us to offer our services to the Church. While committing ourselves, we discover that strength in gentleness and daring in charity of accomplishing the mission begins with him.

Let's pray to him and leave it to Jesus to encourage us to take a step, a small step to help the people who have tasks to do, with humility, in the place where we pray Mass, receive the Word and the Eucharist.

The goal isn't to exhaust the few resources of the few who make themselves available, but to improve the resources that each person has. We're building the local church together in many ways with many people.

One person for the job that ten people could do is very difficult and requires a lot of effort. If we say that nothing happens in the church or that the doors are often locked, what can we do? Who around us, if not ourselves, could offer our services to those in charge?

If ten people do together what a person would usually do alone, let's imagine how it would take away the hassle, the fatigue, and all the opportunities that would arise. Everyone would then be free to evangelize.

May Jesus give us the strength, the courage and the means to work together. Each person is a gift received from God for others. Each person can be directed to an activity of faith to carry out what suits him best.

Let's not be afraid to offer our services to those in charge in the church or in the place near us where mass is held. If they encourage us, it will be so much better. Otherwise, we always have a spiritual service to render, in the meantime, by prayer, for example, and by receiving a formation of faith and evangelization.

God chooses us

Pathway 68

Walking

In the book of Isaiah we read:

"The Lord called me from birth, from my mother's womb he gave me my name."
Isaiah, chapter 49, verse 1

God calls all people, without exception, to a unique vocation and mission. Yet not all people respond to the invitation. Many people don't know it or ignore it or worse yet, refuse to believe it and slow themselves down. Yet it's when we're on the move that we discover the potential of faith that we receive from God.

We are called to a vocation and a mission from our conception. However, we have the freedom to answer yes or no:

"I will make you a light to the nations, that my salvation may reach to the ends of the earth." *Isaiah, chapter 49, verse 6*

Jesus is the Light of the nations and we need his Light to enlighten our faith and to understand the mission. Let's ask him his Light constantly to live well the mission in which he wishes to send us.

Let's walk with the Light of Christ, walk with Christ, walk for Christ, live in Christ and in his Light every day, so that the mission has meaning and fits in God's will. Not my will, but your will, Jesus. It is you, Jesus, who makes us capable of such a beautiful, exciting and wonderful mission.

The Covenant man

It is written:

"On the day of salvation I help you, to restore the land and allot the desolate heritages, saying to the prisoners: 'Come out! To those in darkness: Show yourselves!'" *Isaiah, chapter 49, verses 8 to 9*

"I help you" can be understood as: "I set you apart. I have released you from your habits, distractions that surround you to offer you a mission that you accept freely and that resembles you." Then I make you, "the man of my Covenant".

Note that people who have bright faith "restore the land". It's all the members together that help lift the country. The Lord makes of us the people who work to build bridges between him and humans. Yes, the person who reads this, it is to you that the Lord speaks.

We can see three people in this last part of the text. The first is easy, it's Jesus. Then, the Pope builds bridges between us and God, to introduce us into the Eternal Covenant. Then there are we who are also sent to build bridges between us and God, physically and spiritually. And we'll all say with God, "to the prisoners: 'Come out!' and 'Come to the light'!"

There are already many people who are prophets and answer God's call. Ah! if everyone let their hearts be formed to become prophets, the face of the Church would be radiant! Prophets close to the hearts of the people and who announce the Love, the joy, the mercy, the peace and the hope of God.

As a goal and achievement, the sheep will be well guarded:

"Along the ways they shall find pasture, on every bare height shall their pastures be." *Isaiah, chapter 49, verse 9*

People will have food, drink and light because they will find themselves in the field of God, right now, during their life, and for eternity. Jesus tells us:

"As the Father raises the dead and gives life, so also does the Son give life to whomever he wishes." *John, chapter 5, verse 21*

Jesus is the only one who can find the lost sheep, raise it up and take it in his arms. Jesus transforms the person who is trapped in an obvious death pattern and brings him back to life.

We want to say yes to Jesus, in order to follow the path that leads into the Covenant, to the ultimate encounter with the Trinity.

Jesus adds this truth:

"It was not you who chose me, but I who chose you and appointed you to go and bear fruit that will remain." *John, chapter 15, verse 16a*

We did not choose God, God chose us. Let's keep God in our hearts and in the hearts of those around us. It is now. He's here in our heart.

God is present. He manifests himself in every person. The challenge and the joy we receive is to observe how God lets himself be revealed in them. It's a beautiful mission that Jesus offers us today to listen and to observe his presence manifest by different ways in hearts. The joy that we'll receive will become lifelong jubilation.

To find the gifts and charisms of faith in us and in them is to find God himself. It's also learning and appreciating who he is, in the heart of each person.

The danger

It must have been so difficult for the people who know Jesus to recognize him in his new mission. Jesus changed according to their eyes. From one day to the next, Jesus is on a mission and he must be very different before them. He says and he does what others can't do.

They perceive here and there fragments of what Jesus realizes and it's difficult to place the few pieces of the puzzle in a frame, especially when there are many missing pieces. In addition, they may receive conflicting messages of what they hear about Jesus.

Even today, the ambient message about Jesus, in general, in the world, is sometimes discordant. But it's sometimes easy to trust the fears, rather than what Jesus tells us and realizes.

The people from his home, watching him go, came to seize him because they said:

"He is out of his mind." *Mark, chapter 3, verse 21*

They want to protect their idea of Jesus. They can't imagine for a moment that Jesus entered another stage of his life.

It's a bit like that when a person causes problems in an environment. If people don't check the foundation of a person's mission, fear may be taking hold of some people and it may further harm the mission, instead of helping to build a more just, better world, more merciful and true.

If we begin, in the immediate future, a mission in the name of Jesus, there is a good chance that our surroundings will find us different. It's also possible that some people won't recognize who we are, since we're experiencing a transformation by following Jesus. It is a sign that we're moving forward and a testimony of our faith to them.

Let's give them some time to join us and understand, in faith. Let's pray that they will also discover Jesus in their hearts. Let's give them time to adjust to this novelty.

It's then necessary to meet with other people who have faith in Jesus, to truly enter the mission that allows us to live and achieve goodness.

Let's listen, discern, then encourage and help those who evangelize honestly in the name of Christ, with Christ.

Humility

The judgment

Paul is right:

"The kindness of God would lead you to repentance." *Romans, chapter 2, verse 4*

… To conversion. By and large, Paul invites us to patience, and to receive from people their kindness and generosity. We discover God's goodness in them. The goodness of God overcomes reluctance and attracts to conversion. The call that God sends us is related to his kindness.

He also talks to us about this:

"By the standard by which you judge another you condemn yourself, since you, the judge, do the very same things." *Romans, chapter 2, verse 1*

It must be said that we tend to mix judgment about others with what is a constructive judgment.

Judging others about whom they are at first sight, without really knowing them, is a judgment. But, to observe the actions of another person in order to help, even if we have the same difficulty as this person, can still help.

We must not wait to be perfect to evangelize and help others. Otherwise, nothing would be possible for the world.

And this phrase said by some people sometimes blocks us: "Ah, and you, you are perfect!" In fact, the person may not want our help. We still can pray for him.

Let's face it, nobody's perfect. It would be a shame not to be able to help the people considering that we're also imperfect. Where would charity unfold in such circumstances? It would be like telling a doctor who has cancer that because of that he cannot heal us. We would tell him to heal himself before thinking of healing us. Yet, helping helps to improve who we are. We help each other to help each other, and so on.

Jesus seems to be leading the idea further, when he says to the pharisees:

"You pay no attention to judgment and to love for God." *Luke, chapter 11, verse 42*

That's the basis. A testimony must encourage good deeds. And Jesus brings us back to reality, respectfully. In fact, we're not perfect, and it's clear that our actions and words are not always the best.

What Paul wants us to understand, mostly, is that we cannot evangelize if we're not connected with Jesus. Jesus abounds here, in the same sense. We are invited to deeply convert if we want to evangelize others, but let's not wait to be perfect.

It would be illusory, in spite of our difficulties, not to evangelize when we have received so much, received all from the Lord. Let's trust and evangelize, according to our resources and abilities, according to the openness of our heart. May we remember that it isn't we who evangelize, but Jesus through us.

By improving our life of faith with Jesus, we're on the move. By helping others to improve their lives of faith, we will come closer to Jesus together. Let's destroy our illusions and let God Love us, and through us, let him Love others.

All that we say, all that we achieve will be to lead us and draw people to salvation in the Lord's life.

Let's read a few times what Peter says in this little text and we will have a synthesis of the purpose of our faith:

> "That the genuineness of your
> faith, more precious than gold that
> is perishable even though tested
> by fire, may prove to be for praise,

glory, and honour at the revelation of Jesus Christ. Although you have not seen him you love him; even though you do not see him now yet believe in him, you rejoice with an indescribable and glorious joy, as you attain the goal of (your) faith, the salvation of your souls."
1 Peter, chapter 1, verses 7 to 9

All that we say, all that we realize will be to lead us and lead people to salvation in the kingdom of God. As soon as we direct our life to make it pleasing to God, we also help our neighbour to discover the purpose of life. We walk on the path of holiness.

This passage from Peter is revealing: "As you attain the goal of (your) faith, the salvation of your souls". The salvation of souls is the goal of our faith. It is the will of God and "genuineness of our faith". As soon as a few people come together in the name of Jesus Christ, there will be other people interested in discovering the reality of their faith, and in doing so fulfilling the Lord's mission.

Help people

Let's focus on this passage:

"Refuse no one the good on which he has a claim when it is in your power to do it for him." *Proverbs, chapter 3, verse 27*

This sentence is surprising. Often, we think that we should never refuse our help. It's full of common sense. But there are two nuances here.

The first nuance is that we should not refuse our help to someone, "which he has a claim". Who deserves our help? Let's say that each person deserves our help and deserves to find the Lord.

It might be easier to understand it as follows: "Where it is possible for us to help a person and we're able to do so, let's help them, whether they deserve it or not."

The second nuance is wise: "when it is in your power to do it". We're not told to become needy to help or offer what is not ours, such as material, but to know how to recognize our personal resources and help as best we can, at the best of who we are. With discernment, we will know the percentage of what we can offer, if not everything. It is, however, enjoyable to share the graces that God gives us. They are always available, totally.

When we develop the service resources we have in us, we become more willing and effective in our interventions. Acknowledging our strengths and weaknesses is also a blessing within ourselves. Just thinking about it, we start helping ourselves.

We have only few resources. But together, when we form a helping group, we develop the resources and skills to better help others.

In the end, we must help our neighbour. But we must also know our strengths and limitations. Otherwise, we may be hurting more than we're helping. But this should not stop us from trying to help others in the best way we can. May we accept to learn at our own pace and be more precise of what we can offer. We do not all have the same resources, but our resources are used when they are well used and shared.

Jesus illuminates our lantern:

"No one who lights a lamp conceals it with a vessel or sets it under a bed; rather, he places it on a lampstand so that those who enter may see the light." *Luke, chapter 8, verse 16*

When we pray and deepen our faith through readings and teachings, the Light of Christ will go through our life to enlighten us.

The following may seem surprising:

"To anyone who has, more will be given, and from the one who has not, even what he seems to have will be taken away." *Luke, chapter 8, verse 18*

Let's put this sentence before the light of God. He who receives Light through his relationship with God will enlighten more, since God will come through him for the good of his people. It becomes like the stained-glass windows of a church, illuminated by the sun. He allows the Light of the Trinity to pass through him.

But the person who's not walking or even slowing down and moving away from the Light of God, he even loses the glimmer of what he thinks to hold back for himself.

Let's let God's Light shine in us so that receiving the best from him becomes light for our contemporaries. Let's find ways to keep up with Jesus. It will be a wise step into the Light, as the rays of the sun pass through the clouds.

Humility

Paul tells us:

"Nor, indeed, did we ever appear with flattering speech, as you know, or with a pretext for greed - God is witness - nor did we seek praise from human beings, either from you or from others." *1 Thessalonians, chapter 2, verses 5 to 6*

We are christians, we never need to look for honours. This is interesting to find out if we are walking in the Lord's will. These are christian values to place in our suitcase, for the road.

It's too easy to take ourselves for someone else and not be ourselves. It's easy to get into characters that are successful, that we see on TV or that we hear singing, and stop being ourselves. But the way of another person will never be our own personal way. We will never walk in his shoes.

We must not seek to build our personal kingdom, it would be wrong. We already have everything in the Kingdom of God:

"Happy those who (…) who enjoys the law of the Lord is their joy; God's law they study day and night. They are like a tree planted near streams of water, that yields its fruit in season." *Psalm 1, verses 1 to 3*

To reach wisdom that comes from God, may we let God be God in our life. Better still, may we don't rely on our own strength and let the wisdom of God pass through.

For that, let's become very good friends of God. May we recognize the difference between our thinking and that of Jesus. Let's become more and more filled with his presence. May we know when it is us or Jesus speaking through us.

By the way, we know when we're talking or the person next door is talking. It should be the same for Jesus who goes through our words. We know when our thoughts come from Jesus or from us. There's a difference.

Peter's humility

Our first Pope is full of humility:

"When Peter entered, Cornelius met him and, falling at his feet, paid him homage. Peter, however, raised him up, saying, 'Get up. I myself am also a human being.'" *Acts, chapter 10, verses 25 to 26*

Even if Peter is the Pope whom Jesus has chosen, he knows his rightful place. Already in the Church that is beginning to form, Peter is aware that Jesus continues to be Lord and God. It's amazing!

Peter knew Jesus and lived with him. He was appointed by him the head of the Church. He's also responsible for the Apostles. He has all the reasons to "brag about", to become proud and to become someone else.

For every missionary, Peter has just realized an important teaching with a testimony worthy of a Pope. He sees Cornelius coming and throwing himself at his feet. He could say, "You're a good disciple," or "get up now and let's have a drink".

But by his words, Peter presents himself in a different way. He said to Cornelius, "Get up. I myself am also a human being."

What a beautiful grace of humility! May we ask this grace to Jesus. By his gesture and words, he helps Cornelius to understand that Jesus is Lord. Peter recognizes himself as a simple man and therefore gives full opening to Jesus. He evangelizes.

Peter cannot do anything by himself and he knows it. He's on a mission, but not for himself. He's a missionary for Jesus, for the announcement of the Good News.

Calling all

Peter reminds people that God doesn't categorize between men:

"In every nation whoever fears him and acts uprightly is acceptable to him." *Acts, chapter 10, verse 35*

God rejoices with the people who recognize him as Love. The love of the person is there to join the Love of his Creator. Both are made to live together. God is waiting for love in return for his Love.

His people are so attentive to Peter that they receive the Holy Spirit:

"'Can anyone withhold the water for baptizing these people, who have received the holy Spirit even as we have?' He ordered them to be baptized in the name of Jesus Christ." *Acts, chapter 10, verses 47 to 48*

By their witness of faith, Peter recognizes that they are ready to receive Baptism.

We are made for God

John reminds us that we're made for the Love of God:

"Everyone who loves is begotten by God and knows God." *1 John, chapter 4, verse 7*

He goes so far as to say that we know God when we are born of him and especially if we love … of his Love. John continues:

"In this is love: not that we have loved God, but that he loved us and sent his Son as expiation for our sins." *1 John, chapter 4, verse 10*

John offers an evolution of thought and allows us to better understand how we know God. It was not we who loved God first. We have received the Love of God without even knowing, without asking it. Then we know God as soon as we're aware that all Pure, True, Real Love comes from him.

It's impossible to pull out a single passage in the Bible and think we understand everything. It's like getting married and thinking that everything is successful in the couple, or to receive a baby and say that there's nothing more to achieve for him, since the goal is reached. The baby would come into the world and we would move on. It would be absolutely inconceivable. And this is also true for a relationship with the Word of God. We never stop to know someone and learn with them.

We're improving

The couple's challenge is that each person has his own rhythm and definition of love. The ideal is that each person of the couple improves in the faith. Jesus will ignite Love as it should be. It takes time for someone to realize it, but the experience will be beneficial.

Moreover, every teaching of faith is for each person in the couple, for each spouse. Marriage will be joyful and holy to the extent that each person advances in faith and improves by contact with Jesus.

Each person is responsible for improving his relationship with God, who will, in turn, give graces, a hundredfold, to the spouses. The opening of each one in the couple allows the grace of God to pass into them. This is the only way of a true journey between spouses.

If each person tries to love the other, it's lost. But if each person connects to God and asks Jesus to go through his heart to love, then there's joy that progresses every day, even without their knowledge. Each person in the relationship will have a good reason to give more to each other. Jesus transforms the relationship between them.

It's the same basis for every personal relationship to Jesus:

"As the Father loves me, so I also love you. Remain in my love." *John, chapter 15, verse 9*

God Loves us. Let's stay in his Love. God Loves us first, we only need to welcome and accept his Love. It sounds demanding, maybe. But there's nothing simpler to achieve than to remain in God's Love. Let's love. It is demanding to stay away.

Abiding in the Love of God allows us to discover and gradually recognize the reason we live, the reason we are created. Sticking to God's Love makes us more and more like him.

We have not acquired anything by ourselves. We're not perfect, but we gradually become "love" thanks to God's "Love". When we accept to approach Jesus, we accept to let ourselves be more Loved by him. It takes us away from evil, fear, anxiety and purifies us, meeting after meeting, with him.

Then Jesus again transmits to us the new commandment which is the same as loving God, which is loving our neighbour. Well, to know God more, it's important that we learn to welcome, to love, even with its differences, our neighbour.

Jesus commands us to love. It is the means to remain in God's Love and to move away from evil, self-sufficiency, pride, withdrawal. This commandment of Jesus is bathed in Love.

The commandment of Love is the summit and ultimate realization of the amazing beings that we are. This commandment is for us. It instructs by the tenderness of God so that we become like Him. This is the greatest, the deepest joy that exists.

When we do a dictation at school, the goal is to succeed as close as possible to the sentence that's taught to us orally. What God tells us also allows us to improve and become like him. The more we listen to the voice of God, the more we become holy.

Let's enter through the door of God's Love by following his command to love our neighbour. May we let ourselves be Loved by

God and by our neighbour. And let God Love us and others.

Only men

To know ourselves to be Loved by God and to let him Love others through us is a miracle in itself. We allow Love to touch people. We understand more and more the will of the Trinity.

A man listens to Paul's words:

"He listened to Paul speaking, who looked intently at him, saw that he had the faith to be healed, and called out in a loud voice, 'Stand up straight on your feet.' He jumped up and began to walk about." *Acts, chapter 14, verses 9 to 10*

In a leap, the man walks! What faith does Paul demonstrate in his Lord and how much he listens to the man's faith that he's brought back on his feet! What seems extinguished in this man was waiting only for a thoughtful look from the Apostle, in the name of Jesus, to set his faith on fire and "give him back his legs" to walk.

Paul discovers gifts he didn't know, perhaps. Paul gives what he receives, the gift of healing, but even more, he receives the gift of perceiving faith in people. Paul saw that this man had faith in the words he said, received from Jesus. The crowd is amazed by what Paul realizes before their eyes:

"When the crowds saw what Paul had done, they cried out in Lycaonian, 'The gods have come down to us in human form.'" *Acts, chapter 14, verse 11*

We can imagine that Paul didn't expect what has just been proclaimed. The danger against faith is to believe that there are gods, idols, even humans who think they take the place of God or give to humans God's place.

This is perhaps the most corrosive tendency that exists against faith, that is, placing our faith in anyone or anything but Jesus. And even worse, thinking about taking ourselves or giving them God's place.

Paul declares his faith by his enlightened reason of the divine Light. He defends himself vividly, immediately, to be a "god" at the whim, to the fantasy of humans. He seems aghast, demolished and he tells them:

"Men, why are you doing this? We are of the same nature as you, human beings." *Acts, chapter 14, verse 15*

Paul is a man like all men. No better, no worse. He did not heal anyone. The good news that Paul conveys is that the human is transformed by faith in Jesus Christ. It's Christ who heals this man. Jesus heals. Paul believes it for saying these words.

Let's look deeper into our hearts and we will understand that only Jesus is God. This is not a healing operated by Paul:

"We proclaim to you good news that you should turn from these idols to the living God, 'who made heaven and earth and sea and all that is in them.'" *Acts, chapter 14, verse 15*

With these words, many converted.

As for Paul, Jesus sends us the Holy Spirit so that we can live with contagious faith. Jesus sends us help, support:

"The Advocate, the holy Spirit that the Father will send in my name - he will teach you everything and remind you of all that (I) told you." *John, chapter 14, verse 26*

Jesus announces that there will be people like Paul to intercede with others:

"Whoever loves me will keep my word, and my Father will love him, and we will come to him and make our dwelling with him." *John, chapter 14, verse 23*

Jesus dwells in Paul to proclaim the truth and the Word with tenacious faith, but with human words. Paul conveys the truth and the Word of Jesus and it is Jesus who heals.

Of all that Jesus teaches it invites us to welcome him, then to understand and live it. Paul understood it very well. We also know holy people now who work according to the will of God.

Let's ask Jesus to adjust our faith to our reason and our reason to our faith, so that we may be more and more in the image of our Saviour and Lord, in the midst of the world into which he sends us.

May Mary walk with us, with her example of faith, so that we may be available and free to fulfill what Christ asks of us, for our salvation, for the salvation of our contemporaries and for the glory of God.

Let's ask daily for the presence of the Holy Spirit on us and on the people we meet and we'll discover how he works in hearts.

Expressions of faith

Pathway 70

Peace to people

Jesus says to the Apostles:

"Blessed are the eyes that see what you see. For I say to you, many prophets and kings desired to see what you see, but did not see it, and to hear what you hear, but did not hear it." *Luke, chapter 10, verses 23 to 24*

We're sent to our contemporaries, not to say the same words as them just to make them comfortable, but by speaking a different language. If it's possible for us to get used to their language, it's also possible for them to get used to the language of faith and reason.

We can see Jesus in our hearts and receive our mission from him. Let's ask him to help us prepare ourselves and to illuminate the mission, so that we may walk and evangelize with his words.

Let's pray that our moods and attitudes become holier, so that we may remain peaceful people for ourselves and for those we meet.

Adjusted to the heart

It takes effort not to judge. Let's try not to look at the person only from the outside.

We're invited to pray and love Jesus who's in the person. To love his beautiful talents, his beautiful values, good gestures, good words and to encourage him. To love with Jesus, simply.

Some said to him:

"The disciples of John fast often and offer prayers, and the disciples of the pharisees do the same; but yours eat and drink." *Luke, chapter 5, verse 33*

This distinction is important for us today. In the days of the pharisees, there are norms and laws. It must appear by the actions of all.

And they wonder about the lack of this custom of Jesus's disciples.

We see the break between the old and the New Law. It isn't so much by external practices that the human is saved, but first by the heart. The external practice must be adjusted to the heart. Jesus knows the heart.

Let's become more ourselves and afterwards we can talk and walk with people. We will be able to carry out activities that will lead to Jesus and we will be on a path of conversion.

Let's read this:

> By manifesting Christ the Church reveals to men the real truth about their condition and their whole calling, since Christ is the source and model of that redeemed humanity, imbued with brotherly love, sincerity and a peaceful spirit, to which they all aspire. *Vatican Council II. Ad Gentes. The dogmatic constitution*

on the missionary activity of the Church, number 8.

May the faithful in the Church manifest the presence of Christ in a genuine way so that the world may become more fraternal, renewed, sincere and peaceful. This is what thirsting for truth, respect and reality means.

Paul is on the way when he says:

"I am not ashamed of the gospel. It is the power of God for the salvation of everyone who believes: for Jew first, and then Greek." *Romans, chapter 1, verse 16*

The true believer is on the move and advances in faith.

May the Love of the Trinity engulf us and fill us with his Presence. May the Body and Blood of Jesus Christ be together in our heart. May his life impel us to move, to touch the hearts of the people of his Presence.

Since Mary and Joseph were moving to Egypt, let them help us on the path that leads ever closer, then to the Heart of God.

Events and joy

We know how much Paul's mission has been littered with pitfalls and sometimes difficult adventures. The Lord, in a vision, assures him that he's with him. He encourages him:

"Do not be afraid. Go on speaking, and do not be silent, for I am with you. No one will attack and harm you, for I have many people in this city." *Acts, chapter 18, verses 9 to 10*

Paul is surely reassured and he can now continue to evangelize in joy.

Jesus did mention to the Apostles that the mission wasn't so easy:

"Amen, amen, I say to you, you will weep and mourn, while the world rejoices; you will grieve, but your grief will become joy." *John, chapter 16, verse 20*

We will "weep" and "mourn" "while the world will rejoice". Is there something more difficult when we're in trials that the world rejoices and ignores our trials?

Indeed, this is very difficult, normally. But with Jesus, our lamentations turn into perseverance for the mission. When we're walking with Jesus, we are in joy.

It's when we retreat or we're not walking with Jesus that the discouragement tendency is felt. Let's be reassured, with Jesus and as he told us, our "grief will become joy".

To work, to become the best version of ourselves in the good, the true, the beautiful and the real, doesn't impoverish. This allows us to become more efficient when we invite to conversion.

Let's continue to carry the Holy Spirit in us wherever we go. May the Holy Spirit be our support in trials and our joy in the mission.

Boldness

Paul says to the Corinthians:

"What anyone dares to boast of (I am speaking in foolishness) I also dare." *2 Corinthians, chapter 11, verse 21*

Audacity, we have it all. Many situations in life require a certain amount of audacity. Starting to walk, to talk, to be a teenager, to become an adult, to work, to begin a family, each stage of life requires audacity.

We often see that the audacity of a person can become recklessness or unconsciousness when misused.

On the other hand, audacity allows us to go beyond a usual situation, in order to realize a project that's beyond us. The project of evangelization requires daring.

The audacity of the word is particularly important because it leads to sharing faith when it's credible and attentive to the need of the person. It takes daring to talk to someone:

"If anyone does not fall short in speech, he is a perfect man, able to bridle his whole body also." *James, chapter 3, verse 2*

James also allows us to understand that our words can carry seed of sins. These words would hurt all the best evangelistic initiatives. But the good word edifies people and reveals our good intentions.

Evangelization doesn't tire

Isaiah thought to himself:

"I thought I had toiled in vain, and for nothing, uselessly, spent my strength." *Isaiah, chapter 49, verse 4a*

It would not be surprising that many faith people have this thought someday during their life: "I uselessly spent my strength."

Of course, sometimes we're exhausted, sometimes we feel like going in circles. And even sometimes we run everywhere, in all directions, and we lose time. These are opportunities to learn how to properly manage our efforts and the time we're allowed.

It's important to ask whether Jesus was evangelizing with us, or whether we were all alone. Were we thinking of getting everyone to convert to Jesus, for example, but trying too hard to convert and not enough to unite ourselves to Christ who is the only one who can convert people? Have we placed our trust in Jesus or tried to do his work?

God thinks differently. Isaiah reflects on what God says to him:

"You are my servant, he said to me, Israel, through whom I show my glory." *Isaiah, chapter 49, verse 3*

It's very sweet to the ears: "through whom I show my glory". God passes in us.

It would be important to give ourselves time to meditate and return to the importance of Jesus in our lives, so that Jesus has plenty of room to touch the hearts of those around us. Only Jesus converts.

That's what John the Baptist did. He had a special grace to understand that he isn't the one who transforms hearts, but Jesus is. Evangelization with Jesus doesn't tire.

For John the Baptist:

"The hand of the Lord was with him." *Luke, chapter 1, verse 66*

And:

"The child grew and became strong in spirit." *Luke, chapter 1, verse 80*

From an early age, the faith of John the Baptist was in God and his spirit was united to the Spirit of God. He let himself be filled by grace.

He knew how to recognize his Saviour in Jesus. He pointed toward his direction for the world to convert. His fatigue turns into joy.

John the Baptist did what he could by talking about Jesus and revealing he's the Lamb of God. He left his place so that Jesus may have all the space:

"The next day he saw Jesus coming toward him and said, 'Behold, the Lamb of God, who takes away the sin of the world.'" *John, chapter 1, verse 29*

Let's take a few moments to ask Jesus to take the entire place in our lives and to teach us how to let him convert us each day, so that he may pass through our hearts to convert others. What better mission than to be passers of the faith for the Trinity! Let's let Jesus, the Lamb, care, touch and convert. He knows what he's doing.

Free for Jesus

Paul seems to be proposing a wise phrase to free us from tension and its consequences and keep us in peace as much as possible. By not having too many worries, we will also be freer to walk and follow Jesus:

"The world in its present form is passing away." *1 Corinthians, chapter 7, verse 31*

Time passes, our existence on earth passes. All we currently have is going to stay here. May nothing hold us back, may nothing disturb us.

Sometimes we create our difficulties searching for what we cannot get. But, let's trust in Jesus. All the relationships we have built with people will remain. The love shared and received remains. Let's be happy as we are, with the Trinity. To be happy in God keeps us in reality.

We may have been hurt during our existence, but our existence is not an injury, it's a person. A person Loved by God. A person who, in the present, adjusts to the will and joy of God. Evil and suffering last only in time, our life in God is eternal.

We have a good example when Jesus says, "woe to you". He doesn't make a judgment saying that the person will be unhappy, he rather reveals truth. He knows what remoteness from the Love of God produces:

> But woe to you who are rich, for you have received your consolation. But woe to you who are filled now, for you will be hungry. Woe to you who laugh now, for you will grieve and weep.
> *Luc, chapter 6, verses 24 to 25*

He observes that the person who moves away from the good, the beautiful, the true, the Love of God, becomes unhappy. He becomes unhappy in evil. He's unhappy and he loses his joy. He becomes unhappy, scared. Finally, fear takes over. This fear isn't of God, but the result of a distance from him.

Let's always receive God's joy, let's return to Jesus, in order to remain happy, in spite of the pains and the temporary difficulties of existence.

Take care of yourself

Jesus tells us:

"Love your enemies, and pray for those who persecute you." *Matthew, chapter 5, verse 44*

Jesus especially reminds us that we must look after ourselves, so that we don't enter a game of power and a tortuous path, in order to remain sane. The enemies are doing more harm to themselves. Jesus cares for their hearts. Let's pray for them.

By loving above all, we are invited to observe and listen to the people around us, to nourish them with the Presence of God, to lead them to Christ's Heart.

Our friend

When we have a best friend, we want him to be known. That's why so many people are trying to get Jesus to be known. We stick to him as a friend. And he's God.

There are, however, people who don't know Jesus enough. They think they know Jesus accordingly to some ideas they've gathered. These people will want to eliminate him because he doesn't seem to be like them. He doesn't fit their ideal. Instead of learning to know Jesus better:

"They picked up stones to throw at him."
John, chapter 8, verse 59

May we instead send Jesus flowers and hearts drawn from his Love. May we convert to his Love and become true disciples, following him and for the salvation of the world.

To believe is to escape from confinement. To believe is to learn as a disciple and become an evangelizer.

Night watchmen

There are a lot of people around us who don't know much about their lives. They carry within them secrets which belong to them and which have inhabited most of their lives. At all times, there have been people who have united with the will of God by abandoning what could lead them to bitter pleasures, games of illusions, solicitations of all kinds, which could have captured their spiritual life and lead them out of the path of life, of Love.

These people have moved away from evil and have led us to become watchmen in the night, worshippers of God, walkers for the cause of faith by following Jesus. These people can be our parents, our grandparents, great-grandparents, children, cousins, neighbours, soulmates, friends, especially people who had faith rooted in the Sacred Heart of Jesus.

It is now an opportunity to thank them for their legacy of faith.

Sometimes they were poor at heart and misunderstood. Sometimes they were gentle, but passed for difficult; they cried and they were seen as cry-babies.

They defended justice for a world of love and they could be seen as critics and stubborn; they were merciful and could be considered being too good; pure of heart and they seemed too simplistic; peacemakers and some regarded them as individualistic and distant; sometimes insulted and persecuted for speaking about God. They were right, however, to follow Christ to holiness.

To all these people, we tell you today, thank you. You are in the

"Great multitude" *Revelation, chapter 7, verse 9a*

redeemed by God. You let the Trinity walk and work with you.

On your way, you helped people to follow Jesus under the influence of the Holy Spirit in the Father. The Kingdom of Heaven is yours; you are in the promised land; you are now living satiated, consoled; you bathe in mercy; you are called sons of God; you see God:

"Rejoice and be glad, for your reward will be great in heaven." *Matthew, chapter 5, verse 12*

John is the privileged one, he who saw the open sky. He has a fascinating view of the Son of Man and the woman crowned with twelve stars. John tells us:

"I heard the number of those who had been marked with the seal, one hundred and forty-four thousand marked from every tribe of the Israelites." *Revelation chapter 7, verse 4*

He heard a number. It starts with 144,000, then John is totally surprised to see that there are more saints in the Kingdom of God. He exclaims:

I had a vision of a great multitude, which no one could count, from every nation, race, people, and tongue. They stood before the throne and before the Lamb, wearing white robes and holding palm branches in their hands. *Revelation, chapter 7, verse 9*

Standing! They are alive! They acclaim God! We are also awaited in the open arms of the Trinity who has never ceased to be with us at every moment of our lives: "a great multitude, which no one could count, from every nation, race, people, and tongue. They stood before the throne and before the Lamb" during their life. Now they are in bliss. Happy with Pure, True, Total Love, who hasn't lied to them, who is genuine, delectable and who carries them in his Trinitarian Heart.

Now John speaks to us:

> Beloved, we are God's children now; what we shall be has not yet been revealed. We do know that when it is revealed we shall be like

him, for we shall see him as he is. Everyone who has this hope based on him makes himself pure, as he is pure. *1 John, chapter 3, verses 2 to 3*

Let's ask Jesus to give us strength, courage and audacity to continue in faith, looking toward his Sacred Heart. May his heart overflow from ours. May we gather what we need for evangelization and share its overflow with the people around us.

May Mary and Joseph, with all the saints, known and unknown to us, who are in Bliss in God the Father, the Son, and the Holy Spirit, share in us their joy of being beloved children of the All-Loving Heart of God.

Watch over us

"Keep watch over yourselves and over the whole flock of which the holy Spirit has appointed you overseers, in which you tend the church of God that he acquired with his own blood." *Acts, chapter 20, verse 28*

This recommendation is for all those responsible for at least one person and his journey.

We are reminded of Cain's words to God, right after he killed his brother Abel. The Lord says:

"'Where is your brother Abel?' Cain replied, 'I do not know. Am I my brother's keeper.'" *Genesis, chapter 4, verse 9*

Every person in the Church has the responsibility to help at least one person to discover the good news in Jesus Christ and help them become disciples of Jesus. Jesus acquired members by his own blood. Let's prepare believers for the meeting with him.

We are invited to the same mission. No matter who we are, we are sent into the world, so that the world knows Jesus and discovers God's Love for them. We are the guardians of our brothers, of humanity, of the family of God.

Jesus is at the heart of a great prayer to his Father:

"They do not belong to the world any more than I belong to the world. Consecrate them in the truth. Your word is truth." *John, chapter 17, verses 16 to 17*

We came out of the worldly, we are in the Church, but we also work in the world and we chose to walk with Jesus. Jesus asks the Father to lead us further in his truth. We can also ask for it. The more we are in God's truth, the more our life will offer the testimony of the Father's will.

Jesus wants us to be united in the same mission, with him, for the glory of God and the salvation of the world.

The time we have

According to the book of Haggai, here's a message for us today. The Lord says that these people say that:

"Not now has the time come to rebuild the house of the Lord." *Haggai, chapter 1, verse 2*

Can we afford to slow down the building of the Church? What is most important to us? What do we set as a goal, as a priority?

We have our occupations, our activities, our family and personal obligations and that's very good.

But as the Lord asks, what is the time we have for building the kingdom of God on earth, for his church and for promoting his presence in the hearts? What time do we have left? We have a moment to turn to the Sacred Heart of Jesus. And to ask for help to the Immaculate Heart of Mary.

There is charity, sharing, welcome, joy, love, peace. All this is offered to us free of charge. This, and more, is part of the legacy of faith. As soon as we continue to approach God, all this increases in us and shines on our surroundings.

Thus declares the Lord of the universe [Here is one of his commandments, one of his recommendations]:

"Consider your ways! Go up into the hill country; bring timber, and build the house That I may take pleasure in it and receive my glory, says the Lord." *Haggai, chapter 1, verses 7 to 8*

God is pleased that we are giving him more and more space in our lives. He also enjoys the fact that the Church needs more and more space to contain the multitude of believers who will walk into it.

We improve

Jesus offers a beautiful parable with the tree and its fruits. He said to his disciples:

> A good tree does not bear rotten fruit, nor does a rotten tree bear good fruit. For every tree is known by its own fruit. For people do not pick figs from thornbushes, nor do they gather grapes from brambles.
> *Luke, chapter 6, verses 43 to 44*

God created us good and Jesus speaks to us as God, since he is. He compares us to a tree. We understand that a tree that's not healthy will not give good fruit. And we will do everything to recover the tree, prune it or improve the soil in which it finds its nutrients. If this tree doesn't grow, it will die.

Jesus speaks especially of our faith. For humans, to grow in God is to believe in him! God has created us Love and his Love is to be shared. If a tree held its sap, the branches could not sap the fruit. If the roots of the tree are not planted firmly in the soil, the tree will wobble and fall out of its roots.

The Love we receive wants to be shared. If we retain Love (sap), we stifle the gestures and words that are there to help others. And if we waver for lack of a solid foundation in the faith, we become fragile and ready to be uprooted.

God asks us to share for free what we receive for free. Even the little baby evangelizes, he offers the fruits he receives. And he gives hope that one day his beautiful and good fruits will be picked. There is no age, no specific time to share between us the Love of God who is in us. By sharing what God offers us, the sap of his Love flows in us and offers its fruit to the people who find and pick it.

Help us Jesus

Jesus has a question that shakes:

"Why do you call me, 'Lord, Lord,' but not do what I command?" *Luke, chapter 6, verse 46*

What the mouth says is what overflows the heart if the heart is free, if there's no wall built around it. I ask you to love and you don't, Jesus seems to tell us.

What comes out in words from a closed heart is sometimes or often the opposite of the teaching of the Lord. Then what comes out of our mouth is what the world hears. What the world thinks afterwards is that God isn't good only because we don't share his love.

It becomes a false representation against God. We say Lord, but our mouth doesn't proclaim its reality. Not because God is no longer in our heart, but because we block the sap of Love who must find an exit to sanctify us (make us holy).

Paul says he's a sinner. This is the first condition for moving forward in faith. To affirm that we are sinners gives back to God the Lordship that's his:

"I have been mercifully treated." *1 Timothy, chapter 1, verse 13*

God forgave Paul. God also forgives us so that our hearts may be free again and our lips may tell its wonders.

May we share the faith we receive from God. Let's share our joy once more for being free from sin. In this way, we can receive the sap again and the good fruits that flourish from the grace received by faith.

Mary knew how to receive the fruit of God in her through the Holy Spirit. She gave a Fruit that remains. She gave Jesus to the world. She also gathered Jesus, the Fruit, on the tree of the Cross, taking Jesus in her arms after the descent of the Cross. With Mary, we can say:

Happy those who do not follow the counsel of the wicked, Nor go the way of sinners, nor sit in company with scoffers. Rather, the law of the Lord is their joy; God's law they study day and night. They are like a tree planted near streams of water that yields its fruit in season. *Psalm 1, verses 1 to 3*

Let's ask Jesus to help us recognize his good fruit in us. May his Holy Spirit shower us with graces so that our tree of life may grow and give succulent fruits around us, and may the Father rejoice with us.

In reality, the less weight we have on our conscience, the closer we will be to Jesus and participate in the salvation of humanity.

It is by being empty of ourselves that the Lord can act in our lives and in the lives of others by making us the honour of his presence. To be empty of ourselves allows

Jesus to pass more easily through us. The way should be clear.

Especially today, where we are with people, we can continually ask Jesus to join them. Before meeting with a person or in a group, let's ask the Holy Spirit to get ahead of us and reach a particular person.

We can go further in the reflection. The food of heaven is offered to all so we may live the freedom of the children of God. Approaching the Meal of God liberates and nourishes us already from what awaits us in heaven; the sublime food of the Pascal Lamb.

Paul shares with us the reality that already awaits us as we approach the Body and Blood of Christ:

"God has now reconciled in his fleshly body through his death, to present you holy, without blemish, and irreproachable before him." *Colossians, chapter 1, verse 22*

May we become friendlier with God and be near people. This is the foundation of the mission. To evangelize, to share what comes from God, let's join him.

Paul is too inflamed

The Church in foundation is missionary. Even today, she's missionary. People unite with the Apostles and become witnesses and Christ's evangelizers. This is what happens with Paul.

Paul seeks to enter the group of disciples, but they know him and they're afraid of him. They heard that he was persecuting christians.

Paul lives his poverty. He has a past that follows him and the new-born christian community is well advised. He just converted, but with good reason, fear had seized christians because of the persecution it was subjected to.

So, when Paul comes near the christian camp, they don't want to see him:

"They were all afraid of him, not believing that he was a disciple." *Acts, chapter 9, verse 26*

Paul, of himself, cannot approach christians so easily. We imagine how difficult it is for them to receive and welcome him. We can imagine their questioning. Will he persecute them again?

Barnabas, Paul's friend and a convinced christian, recognizes Paul's peculiar poverty. He recognizes that Paul's past betrays who he is now. He knows that he has changed, that he has become a real witness of faith in Jesus Christ. Now, Barnabas helps him to connect with christians in Jerusalem.

It's not always easy to accept a new person. It takes a little discernment. Paul is newly converted. He therefore needs a friend who's already in the primitive community of Christians and can introduce him to others:

> Then Barnabas took charge of him
> and brought him to the apostles,

and he reported to them how on
the way he had seen the Lord and
that he had spoken to him, and
how in Damascus he had spoken
out boldly in the name of Jesus.
Acts, chapter 9, verse 27

Barnabas's friendship allows Paul to find his rightful place. If it wasn't for Barnabas, perhaps Paul would not have succeeded alone in breaking through the wall of the resistant christian community.

Barnabas says that Paul preaches with assurance. This confirms that Paul lived a conversion, he has a personal relationship with Jesus. He has faith and is very comfortable talking about him. He easily shares his faith in the streets.

We know that Paul evangelized with the passion and determination that is known to him. But Paul may be a little too much on fire:

"He also spoke and debated with the Hellenists, but they tried to kill him." *Acts, chapter 9, verse 29*

New convert, he wants to convert everyone. To convert too much, maybe. Brothers take him aside and send him a little further on the road to Tarsus. They're being careful:

"When the brothers learned of this, they took him down to Caesarea and sent him on his way to Tarsus." *Acts, chapter 9, verse 30*

The real witness

John tells us:

"We have seen and testify that the Father sent his Son as savior of the world." *1 John, chapter 4, verse 14*

John remembers the moments he spent with Jesus. He saw Jesus in his humanity. He spoke with Jesus. John has spent hours listening to him speak. He marvelled at all the good that was done during his stay. He acknowledges it:

"The love of God was revealed to us." *1 John, chapter 4, verse 9*

He saw it, he lived it with Jesus. And he certainly understands that "the Father sent his Son as Savior of the world".

John is a true witness. He's the Apostle of the recognition of the Love of God radiating in Jesus for the salvation of all.

Jesus invites us to trust in Him:

> Amen, amen, I say to you, whoever believes in me will do the works that I do, and will do greater ones than these, because I am going to the Father. And whatever you ask in my name, I will do, so that the Father may be glorified in the Son. *John, chapter 14, verses 12 to 14*

Since Jesus is with the Father and the Spirit, he can act in many people at once. And he can act in the faith of many people by the proclamation, by the evangelization of true witnesses.

However, it's necessary that people agree to be on the move and become friends of the Love of the Trinity for the welfare of many.

Let's be confident as the Virgin Mary and become faithful witnesses who live the faith. Let's reject all that isn't of God and place our heart in the pierced Heart of our Lord and Saviour.

Keep courage

Paul noticed in Timothy some fears concerning the mission. He tells him:

"I remind you to stir into flame the gift of God that you have through the imposition of my hands. For God did not give us a spirit of cowardice but rather of power and love and self-control." *2 Timothy, chapter 1, verses 6 to 7*

Paul is attentive to the faith of those around him.

Sometimes, when everything is going too fast, let's return to what is simple in the faith. He tells us to awaken in us, again, the gift of God. Let's return wholeheartedly to this moment of grace and the mission will continue. Let's stay courageous and trust in Jesus Christ.

Peter forgives

Peter is very active. He says something that needs to be mentioned. He speaks to the people in front of the Temple officials:

"You denied the Holy and Righteous One and asked that a murderer be released to you. The author of life you put to death, but God raised him from the dead; of this we are witnesses." *Acts, chapter 3, verses 14 to 15*

Peter reminds them of their actions. Without telling them about the commandments, they had to think about the consequences of the Ten Commandments, especially not to kill their neighbour. Peter seems to make sure that they understand the meaning of their actions. Then, Peter surprises with his words:

> Now I know, brothers, that you acted out of ignorance, just as your leaders did; but God has thus brought to fulfillment what he had announced beforehand through the mouth of all the prophets, that his Messiah would suffer. Repent, therefore, and be converted, that your sins may be wiped away.
> *Acts, chapter 3, verses 17 to 19*

Peter could have condemned them, in his way, with stinging words, worthy of a brilliant, dramatic and tasty play! But he goes far beyond what he can see and understand in order to touch the hearts of those responsible at the Temple. He even calls them "brothers!"

Then he tells them that their actions were done by ignorance. Peter knows what he's talking about because he himself was often unaware of what Jesus really meant and said.

Peter needed the resurrection to better understand Jesus's reality. Then he recalls that in God's plan it was clearly written that the Messiah would suffer. And he ends with a vibrant invitation. Convert "that your sins may be wiped away".

We convert, turn to God, return to God, it has the same meaning, to be free from our sin.

The story doesn't say whether those Temple officials were baptized. But we can marvel at how Peter is now a complete Apostle. And with what sweetness, delicacy, he addresses these people. He went beyond himself, acted and talked like Jesus. He really received the Light of Christ!

The Spirit frees

Shortly before, Christ blew the Holy Spirit on Peter and the Apostles when they were in a closed room. Jesus spreads his breath on them and say:

"Receive the holy Spirit. Whose sins you forgive are forgiven them, and whose sins you retain are retained." *John, chapter 20, verses 22 to 23*

Jesus goes beyond our understanding by his resurrection. Peter understood it. Jesus adds that he wants:

"That repentance, for the forgiveness of sins, would be preached in his name to all the nations, beginning from Jerusalem." *Luke, chapter 24. verse 47*

This is what Peter testifies before the world and before the temple leaders; he forgives their faults and invites them to conversion. This testimony helps people understand who Jesus really is.

Let's place our trust in Jesus, to believe that he's the Resurrection and Life. Jesus opened for us the gates of Eternal Life and he offers us forgiveness, so that we begin right now to open the door of our salvation and immediately taste the joy and peace there.

Values

The Apostles didn't choose Jesus, Jesus chose the Apostles. God always passes in front of people. Jesus is the Good Shepherd who takes care of us. He watches over us. When he passes in our life, he doesn't pass without realizing what is good. His Love reassures us and fills us with benefits.

As the sun warms us, the sun (Son) of God transforms us by all that is best. He allows us to discover in ourselves what life is, love, truth, joy, faith. God allows us to discover the values that he originally deposited in us.

Let's continue to receive God and let him help us discover his presence in our lives, like thousands of bright, spiritual and comforting jewels that serve to enlighten the world.

Amos says:

"Seek good." *Amos, chapter 5, verse 14*

The more we love and appreciate goodness, the more goodness feeds the world and goes around it. However, evil causes harm.

It is the responsibility of each person to advance the cause of good for humanity. All the chances we get must be at the service of the good. Whenever good is realized, God is with us. It brings us closer to God.

We can try to do activities or beautiful things that can help in a liturgy or to evangelize, that's good, but also, may the Love received from God circulate in our heart, in order to let it spring up and down on the world, it's better. God says:

"Let justice surge like water, and goodness like an unfailing stream." *Amos, chapter 5, verse 24*

Law and justice must always be nourished by the Love of God if we want improvement for the human being. To be right with others, to offer what we receive from God and to be right in our intentions is an advantage.

It is a necessity to properly observe our actions, our behaviour, our attitude, to be fair, right and true. Observation of what we do personally helps us to discern between what is good to do, what is less good and what to leave out.

Sometimes we talk too fast, sometimes we act too fast, sometimes our attitude isn't appropriate. Observation of ourselves can improve relationships with others.

The more Love of God in the world, the more freely this Love flows in human life, the more evil cannot take hold of the human being.

May our life become like Jesus's life, may our heart become like his Heart.

The only good

Jesus tells us:

"Amen, I say to you, you will not be released until you have paid the last penny."
Matthew, chapter 5, verse 26

Just to grasp how the phenomenon of money works in our world, we observe how delicate it is and how people, in general, don't like to do wrong by counting money. That sometime exceeds us, seizes us.

Moreover, we all feel bad when we think we can't give the right amount to a person, or not having the right amount at the end of the budget exercise and worse, the closure of the budget of a company for which we work for. It could cost a lot and demand of us extra hours of work.

Money is an important factor in what Jesus tells us because it invites us to vigilance and a particular and rigorous attention. But Jesus cannot tell us this without thinking about sharing something wider, deeper.

As Jesus says:

"Unless your righteousness surpasses that of the scribes and Pharisees, you will not enter into the kingdom of heaven." *Matthew, chapter 5, verse 20*

This justice must come from Jesus. May we ask him for it. His justice is based on Love, because everything that hurts love hurts people and harms our relationship with God. Justice is to give back to others what is necessary, what he needs and which comes from God, firstly.

As for money, we learn to be precise, but generous with our way of sharing the Love we receive from God. To love our neighbour says a lot about the quality of the relationship we have with Jesus and the amount of Love we absorb from him.

The only true way to be fair and honest in receiving and sharing the Love of Jesus is to ask everything of him, and to be instructed on the nature of his Heart.

Then, justice, the love received from Jesus becomes the only good that we need to share in all the encounters we experience, in all the relationships that allow us to share what we have received in abundance.

Let's be happy

Pathway 71

Smile

We cannot imagine all the joy our life can hold to know that our Saviour, the Lord whom we want to follow, is the summit of hope in the world. Let's imagine the greatest joy that exists and yet we haven't grasped the striking sweetness of God's joyful Heart:

"Shout for joy, O daughter Zion! sing joyfully, O Israel! Be glad and exult with all your heart, O daughter Jerusalem!" *Zephaniah, chapter 3, verse 14*

This daughter of Zion represents Mary. This girl from Jerusalem has every reason to rejoice, to shudder with joy. She bears the Saviour.

Sometimes people ask, "Why are you smiling?" It's like our smile is suspicious or it seems to hide something, or we seem to be wasting time. The smile is lauded in advertisements to sell products. But it's hardly acceptable in society.

The smile isn't valued enough. Too often we give it negative motives. Smiling isn't for sale, but to be lived.

We sometimes hear this remark: "This person cannot smile, I know it's not going well in his life." We can therefore perceive the smile as a lie if the person lives a trial and he smiles all the same. Yet even in the midst of the ordeal, joy doesn't suddenly become a stranger to a person's heart.

The smile of the heart is a sign of a different joy, a superior joy, an entire joy that comes from God. It would be nice to find ways to encourage people to smile.

If joy raises questions for some, it doesn't mean that a person doesn't have moments of suffering, worry or pain. He's similar in nature to his neighbour. It doesn't mean that he doesn't care about others. But he knows how to find and feel deep joy in the core of his being.

We can have so much joy, that it can happily become unbearable. It's offered to everyone. It's hard to receive so much joy, since we're not used to letting it go.

We can offer this excess of joy to Jesus for another person or ask him to keep it for later, so that we may remain in joy and pass it on to the hearts that need it: "Shout for joy, O daughter Zion! sing joyfully, O Israel! Be glad and exult with all your heart, O daughter Jerusalem!"

Why would it be otherwise? If we believe that God is Love and a manifestation of Love is joy, let's pay more attention to joy that springs from our heart.

During a sports game, when our team counts, we shout out of joy! Why is it possible to celebrate in an arena and that we are choked to do it in simple situations of life as for a new realization, for an effort of prayer and sharing? There are so many opportunities to let our joy out. All this love of God that we carry in our heart seeks to spread its wings to fly over people and groups, and hope to rejoice in hearts.

Paul tells us:

"Rejoice in the Lord always. I shall say it again: rejoice!" *Philippians, chapter 4, verse 4*

Thank you, Paul! Well said. Let's always be in joy or at least let's always reveal the joy in us. This doesn't prevent the .5% of our life that goes wrong, but we have the right to live in joy:

"In everything, by prayer and petition, with thanksgiving, make your requests known to God," *Philippians, chapter 4, verse 6*

continues Paul. In joy, thanksgiving, let's work with the Lord. Let's keep joy alive.

John the Baptist prepared the crowd for the coming of our Lord Jesus, we can also prepare hearts by contagious joy. We don't need to develop, to force joy, we only need to find it in our heart and transmit it.

We are saturated with joy and what hurts us is to not let it out, or that others don't welcome it. But, at least, let's let it out. Maybe they will become more familiar to it.

The presence of Jesus in Mary is the joy of Joseph, Elizabeth and John the Baptist. Mary is also the reason for our greatest joy, since the joy in her is God. Jesus is the bearer of joy. He invites us to happiness.

May joy spread like dew, so that the world around us may believe in a more beautiful life filled with hope.

Someone will say, "Yes, but there's war in the world!" Of course. But the more joy there is in the world, the more peace will spread and fewer wars there will be. Isn't that reasoning good enough?

Let's allow moments with the Lord to feel his joy invade us.

Watch over faith

Paul offers us a warning:

"Let's be on our guard while the promise of entering into his rest remains, that none of you seem to have failed." *Hebrews, chapter 4, verse 1*

This is another way of saying, "Watch over us and the neighbour."

God promises us eternal rest, eternal life, and there are fears that we may be a little late, or even miss out on it. Let's watch over our faith and at the same time discover ways to watch over the faith of others.

First, by watching over our personal faith, we offer ourselves opportunities to leap into holiness to enter the Kingdom of God. Then, while making sure to encourage the faith of others, we allow others to taste eternal joys now. Living in faith is the way of already feeling the opening of heaven's door.

By helping others, we at the same time solidify our own faith. We practise our faith when we find ways to share it. By transmitting the joy of faith, we help people to know God.

To regroup in prayer is necessary to join the faith of people who seek, but have not yet found Jesus. And who knows, Jesus can offer healing to those who discover faith if they want.

Good fruits

Jesus tells us:

"Just so, every good tree bears good fruit, and a rotten tree bears bad fruit. (...) So by their fruits you will know them." *Matthew, chapter 7, verses 17 and 20*

We could say that all the trees that give fruit are good trees. And it's true, in general, all fruit trees give very good and tasty fruit.

If the tree is not connected to a source, it will not be able to bear good fruit. Place a fruit tree in a rock quarry, it won't offer fruit and it will die.

It's at this moment that discouragement follows. We sometimes wonder why nothing is working out. The answer is related to our relationship to God. Are we too far from him?

Jesus is always going deeper with what he tells us. He doesn't just talk about trees. Whenever we read about Jesus, let's be assured that he invites us to go further and deeper. Jesus speaks of the heart which is the crib of bearing fruit. Our heart can bear good fruit or we block the source (Jesus) and there will come out bad fruit.

It's disturbing to know that we can bear bad fruit. There are also poisonous fruits that can kill people. But the time we spend improving in the Lord prevents evil from settling and hurting ourselves, thus hurting others. Good fruits feed happiness, joy.

Jesus gave us a law to develop good fruit. It is to love one another, because by loving, we allow the Love of God to pass through the fibres of our being and our heart. May our life be connected to God's Source to the extent that we let his Love pass through for the world.

As the sap rises in the tree to give good fruits, the Love of God must find its place in our life, so that we receive it in abundance and that we become caring loving people.

When we are in the Lord, the fruits of faith progress. The more we please ourselves in God's law, the more we will discover what his Love will do in us and the more we will know how to share it as the tree shares its fruit without trying to hold them back.

The tree becomes totally destitute when it's time to gather its fruits. He does not hold them back, though sometimes his branch seems to want to hold them back. He offers them to us and we only need to pick and choose them. Let's become so poor that the fruits we carry are rightfully picked. Let's look for the pickers who are looking for the fruits that God is growing in our tree, in our being.

With God, all we have to do is let ourselves be watered by his Source of Love, let his sap pass through us, grow in faith and share the fruits at harvest time.

Let's be vigilant and ready

Jesus shares with his disciples:

> Be sure of this: if the master of the house had known the hour when the thief was coming, he would not have let his house be broken into. You must also be prepared, for at an hour you do not expect, the Son of Man will come. *Luke, chapter 12, verses 39 to 40*

Often, we have understood this statement of Jesus as if God is coming to cut the tree, to pull us out of life like a thief. We think that God decides when he comes to pick us up, when he will need us in heaven or because he coldly decides that our time has passed like the last grain of sand in the hourglass of time. It's an image too imperfect for God who is so perfect.

Once again, let's go beyond the initial understanding we have of God's intention. God is Love. And since God is Love, he Loves us. God is here from the beginning of our life. He welcomes us into his family at the moment of our baptism and he's also present at the moment we of the return to his home.

If Jesus speaks of the thief who can surprise us, it's because he wants us to be always ready to search, see and to meet him. The Trinity wishes that our heart is already in relation with him, in order to recognize him when he invites us to follow him, when he invites us to the mission, when he invites us to holiness. For holiness is lived walking with Jesus and not away from him.

Let's live in faith, to recognize Jesus when we come to the Kingdom. Because, in reality, there is no thief when we are aware of Jesus's presence in our life, when we are on the path and we live small regular conversions of the heart:

"Peter said, 'Lord, is this parable meant for us or for everyone?'" *Luke, chapter 12, verse 41*

Do I have to always be ready like this Jesus? Must I always be attentive to your Presence in me and in the world? Do I have to watch over everyone?

Certitude and passion

Jesus answers Peter:

"Blessed is that servant whom his master on arrival finds doing so." *Luke, chapter 12, verse 43*

In simple, it means: "Let's be vigilant and ready."

People who want to follow Christ are in his mission. They agree to follow Christ to become like him, active for all, without exception.

Jesus will accompany us, he is patient and ready to feed us with what's necessary for the mission. He wants us to be on the road going toward people who are eager to know him and to awaken faith in people who don't know him.

Jesus wants us to move forward in faith and joy as servants who know their teacher and speak about him with certainty and passion.

The worst danger would be to fight for faith by hurting, being negative, defeatist, having proud expectations and confronting the Church and the world. It would be contrary to the will of God.

Let's rather advance in trust in the Church founded by Jesus Christ, placed in the hands of the Apostles and in their successors the bishops, in this Church, which is led by the Holy Spirit, according to the Father's will.

God entrusts his mission

Then to the one who transmits the Gospel:

"He will put him in charge of all his property." *Luke, chapter 12, verse 44*

All goods received from the Love of God. What joy!

The Trinity will entrust everything to those who dare to enter the march of saints by sharing their faith in Jesus Christ for the salvation of the world and for the glory of God.

Prayer elevates us to God and protects us in the spiritual struggle between good and evil. It keeps us focused on the will of God. Happy are those who watch in prayer and work in the following of Christ for a world of peace, joy, hope and love.

Good intentions

It's easy to let tensions that we live rise in us, give them words and that those words go wrong. Sometimes, we can be caught through these for years. We all have seen one day at home or in someone else words and phrases that are useless, overwhelming and sometimes heartbreaking.

Here is Paul's testimony:

"You heard of my former way of life in Judaism, how I persecuted the church of God beyond measure and tried to destroy it." *Galatians, chapter 1, verse 13*

Bad habits, remoteness of the Good News and from the will of God leads people to increase tensions, even to persecute, without being aware of the weight they place on other people.

We also observe in families how tensions can easily rise. Whatever we do, whatever we say, the important thing is to return quickly to good intentions.

Let's ask Jesus to journey with us, to help us make meaningful connections with people and to remove all the little roots that could keep us away from the Good News and announced by our actions and words.

To feed on

The essential element of the mission is to strengthen our faith. Taking time to nourish ourselves with the Word and the Eucharist will allow us to continue in faith. It's essential to know more about Jesus who invites us to share the Good News of salvation:

> A Jew named Apollos, a native of Alexandria, an eloquent speaker, arrived in Ephesus. He was an authority on the scriptures. He had been instructed in the Way of the Lord and, with ardent spirit, spoke and taught accurately about Jesus, although he knew only the baptism of John. He began to

speak boldly in the synagogue; but when Priscilla and Aquila heard him, they took him aside and explained to him the Way (of God) more accurately. And when he wanted to cross to Achaia, the brothers encouraged him and wrote to the disciples there to welcome him. After his arrival he gave great assistance to those who had come to believe through grace. He vigorously refuted the Jews in public, establishing from the scriptures that the Messiah is Jesus. *Acts, chapter 18, verses 24 to 28*

To possess the scriptures, to speak with confidence, to expose with greater precision what concerns Jesus, to demonstrate by the Scriptures that Jesus is the Messiah are all terms relating to the mission and evangelization.

Jesus adds:

"Amen, amen, I say to you, whatever you ask the Father in my name he will give you. Until now you have not asked anything in my name; ask and you will receive, so that your joy may be complete." *John, chapter 16, verses 23b to 24*

Jesus says that we have not asked for anything yet. His message is so precious. Let's ask Jesus and we will receive him. He cannot get tired of us or our demands. Let's ask the Father and the Spirit, in the name of Jesus, and we will receive what's needed, according to the will of God. We will thus live, naturally, by whom we want to live.

What we are looking for is an answer in Jesus. But alone, we look elsewhere and we are often disappointed with the results. Let's entrust our lives to Jesus and we will live fully, in a fulfilling way.

Jesus invites us to ask him to pass in us and before us so that he may be known and his good news be exposed to the world. Let's take the time to stand before Jesus and ask him to give us everything we need to share his Love onto others.

Zelie and Louis Martin, Josephine Bakhita, Marguerite of Metola, the saints stood before Jesus to receive everything from him and to live with him.

To let oneself be Loved by God and to let God Love the neighbour by going through us is worth:

"more than all burnt offerings and sacrifices". *Mark, chapter 12, verse 33*

that we can realize by ourselves and which are often a waste of energy and time.

But there is an offering and a sacrifice that pleases God. The offering of the Son on the altar is his sacrifice for our salvation. Jesus Christ is sacrificed for our salvation and he offers himself Body and Blood. Let's trust him.

Through the Eucharist, let's recognize what we receive and what Jesus calls us to live. We have Jesus as model, we can let him inspire us.

During the Eucharist, let's give to Jesus, on the paten, all the people of whom we think of, all the people we have the chance to meet day to day and those we least think of. May Jesus transform their lives, free them from evil, for them to enter into the joy of the Trinity.

To evangelize is easy

Peter believes it and exhorts the presbyters:

"Through Silvanus, whom I consider a faithful brother, exhorting you and testifying that this is the true grace of God. Remain firm in it." *1 Peter, chapter 5, verse 12*

If it is the grace of God that we feel with us, best we stay there, if it isn't the grace of God, let's leap to the grace of God. It's thanks to God that we hold in faith.

Mark, Peter's friend and writer of the 2nd Gospel, remained stuck to the grace of God. And he was allowed to tell us what he knows about Jesus's life. We enjoy the privilege of reading the words and gestures of Jesus that were transmitted to us.

The risen Jesus told the eleven Apostles:

"Go into the whole world and proclaim the gospel to every creature. Whoever believes and is baptized will be saved; whoever does not believe will be condemned." *Mark, chapter 16, verses 15 to 16*

… and the others will be condemned? It's a very harsh reproach to say that others will be condemned, but it isn't Jesus who will condemn them. The person condemns himself by refusing to believe. Let's pray instead of forcing him. For to force conversion can push him deeper into the habit of being away from Jesus.

Each person has common sense. Common sense leads to holiness. Common sense is to walk away from evil for to walk and follow Jesus. To announce him, it takes people who become familiar with the Scriptures and are sent by Christ.

It isn't difficult to evangelize. What becomes complicated is not to be on a mission.

We introduce our friends to people around us? We love Jesus? Let's introduce our friends to Jesus. If people present their friends in bars, sports centres, at work, we can introduce more people to our friend, and his name is Jesus. Then, with a little practice, we can learn to get him known.

Mark had his own way of making Jesus known to us by Scripture. We all have a personal way, united to the will of God, to develop ways for Jesus to be known. Let's ask Jesus to teach us how to discover in ourselves, our way of making him known. Let's be ourselves in the best and holy version of ourselves.

May Mary walk with us on the road. May Jesus be present in the heart of each person. May the grace of Christ transform how we welcome others, and how we will proclaim the gospel.

Announce Jesus

Paul was arrested and he's under interrogation. Governor Festus tells what he knows about him and his friends:

"They had some issues with him about their own religion and about a certain Jesus who had died but who Paul claimed was alive." *Acts, chapter 25, verse 19*

There isn't much difference between what Paul lived and what we live today. We also announce that Jesus died and rose again. It is the basis of our faith. At each Eucharistic celebration, we announce that Jesus has risen from the dead and is constantly with us.

In number *1366 of the catechism*, we find this presentation of the Eucharist: "[Christ], our Lord and God, was once and for all to offer himself to God the Father by his death on the altar of the cross, to accomplish there an everlasting redemption".

Our recognition is declared:

> The Eucharist is a sacrifice of thanksgiving to the Father, a blessing by which the Church expresses her gratitude to God for all his benefits, for all that he has accomplished through creation, redemption, and sanctification. Eucharist means first of all 'thanksgiving'. *Catechism of the Catholic Church, number 1360, website*
>
> *http://www.vatican.va/archive/E NG0015/__P41.HTM*

The Eucharist lives in the present of God, at each Mass.

Peter, Follow Me

Jesus gives Peter his mission, after having asked him three times if he loves him, to take care of his kingdom on earth, of his Church:

"Feed my lambs, (...) Tend my sheep, (...) Feed my sheep." (*See John, chapter 21, verses 15-17*)

The keys are now in Peter's hands, according to the Gospel of John.

Another major point is that Jesus sends Peter on a mission. But he also wants Peter to stay with him. Jesus says to him:

"Follow me." *John, chapter 21, verse 19*

It's as if he said: "Be always with me Peter, I am your reference, your Lord and your God. Follow me! announce the Good News and Baptize in the Name of the Father, the Son and the Holy Spirit, and that all the sheep to whom I send you, first be my sheep, seems to say Jesus." He entrusts them to Peter.

In the race

In the book of Deuteronomy, it is described that Moses passes into eternity and Joshua takes over the people of Israel. Human existence is a relay race with sometimes obstacles, sometimes mountains to climb, sometimes plains to cross, waters to cross. There are also interior deserts to search for the way to go and the voice to convey. We are in this race to share our faith from one person to another.

Even though everything may seem wrong, we can continue to follow Jesus. But also, it is imperative to stand with Jesus even when we are on a good path and everything seems to be going well. Let's not take our relationship with Jesus for granted. We can easily shy away. We are still too fragile and we are not yet at our destination. May grace continue to increase in us.

Jesus said to his disciples:

"If your brother sins (against you), go and tell him his fault between you and him alone. If he listens to you, you have won over your brother." *Matthew, chapter 18, verse 15*

Today we would say; teach the good and the truth in the name of Jesus and watch the people advance in their faith.

Teaching the well-being of faith in Jesus Christ will join people. Then, with their freedom, they will decide to live it out. We are invited above all to let people free, but also to find the best ways, delicate and respectful, without ever rushing, to allow them to taste the joy we live and to know we're saved by Christ.

He who loves God and is Loved by him wishes to transmit Love to others by appropriate gestures and words, always with respect, dignity and the greatest charity.

On a mission

What can lead us to heaven? What allowed Mary to live the Assumption? Jesus ... and her special attention to Jesus. Mary had audacity and she entered the challenge to make of her life, to make of her body a house of prayer. She received Jesus in her and she gave him to others, starting with Joseph.

Jesus, when he was very young, didn't have much choice to follow Mary and Joseph for years. And Mary didn't stop living with Jesus when she was at home or on the road, on the way to the house of her cousin Elizabeth, or in a wedding at Cana, for example.

But what do we have in our homes? Today, we are invaded with many stuff. The internet plays an important role in the establishment of customs in our lives. Even if it isn't internet, there's television or other means to help barricade us in the house, with also certain newspapers, books and music that don't offer many faith solutions.

It may be time to rethink the mission by renewing, bathing our heart in Jesus's.

The more we are going to make our homes and our hearts prayer centres, the more we will increase our faith, then we will feed more people in society.

Let's pray and ask Jesus what we can transform in our homes. How can we open more room for him, where we live most of our days?

There are certainly some who have already found solutions to make their homes a house of prayer, of thanksgiving and attention to God. Every moment of our life can become an instant of prayer. Let's continue to find ways to deepen our faith, and we can say, like Elizabeth, who welcomes Mary into her home:

"And how does this happen to me, that the mother of my Lord should come to me?"
Luke, chapter 1, verse 43

... with the Lord, with Jesus in her! May Mary and Joseph be the patron saints of our home. When they are near us, so is Jesus. Then, widen space for Jesus to live here.

Attitude and Holy Spirit

Paul opens his heart:

"Put on then, as God's chosen ones, holy and beloved, heartfelt compassion, kindness, humility, gentleness, and patience." *Colossians, chapter 3, verse 12*

We have a sign that we are sanctified by God simply by observing in ourselves and in others signs of "holy and beloved, heartfelt compassion, kindness, humility, gentleness, and patience".

When we carry these attitudes of the heart within us, we know that the Holy Spirit has a place in our life. But that doesn't mean that when it's a bit harder, the Holy Spirit is no longer there.

And if we feel less of the Holy Spirit, we can work more on transmitting necessary values to develop from one life to another. We will feel the Spirit again when we are more in movement with him. The Holy Spirit did not go away, he didn't leave, he is here.

Let's work to increase the values in our life and we will become a source of the Holy Spirit for the world. Let's keep the Holy Spirit with us and he will act through us. May the world be filled with his presence and his action for hearts and consciences to be touched for a better world.

Let's look at these next two sentences:

"Rage seizes me because of the wicked; they forsake your teaching." *Psalm 119, verse 53*

We see that this passage dates from another age, before the birth of Jesus Christ. In this context, the ungodly are those who do not believe.

Then, fury is a sad phenomenon that doesn't give many results. Fury is not a good counselor. It's better to live in peace by a charitable action inspired by Jesus and share our faith as we can with humility and hope. Let's place our trust in Jesus.

The second sentence:

"Though the snares of the wicked surround me, your teaching I do not forget." *Psalm 119, verse 61*

This is a good method. When people do not have faith and try to pull us out of reality and then get us into evil, it's good to remember that God watches over us. To have God is all that we need at times of trial. Help will be revealed as needed.

God guarantees us his great mercy and reminds us that humility is a wise attitude to continue to live in faith, despite the contrary winds that sometimes lurk nearby.

For our salvation

Pathway 72

The personal conversion

It is the most beautiful mission that a person can live on earth, it is the greatest work to which the Trinity invites us, what Jesus tells us at this moment:

"As you go, make this proclamation: 'The kingdom of heaven is at hand.'" *Matthew, chapter 10, verse 7*

If we could direct our life and reduce the reason for our life to mere evangelization on the road, to proclaim that "the Kingdom of Heaven is at hand", not only will the people around us have the chance to know Jesus but by our actions and our human means to make him known, we ourselves will have a reason to live faith actively and nourish it every day.

Getting started is the key to our personal conversion. It is also the key to the conversion of people who join us on the road.

The resting peace of believers is realized through evangelization. For when we find Jesus, who is happiness and endless Love, we watch as long as we know he's known.

Let's evangelize in gentleness and respect and we will also evangelize ourselves. We will be patient with ourselves. This step will give us patience.

Let's have one foot in the Church, together, to stick to the Lord's teaching and to make our faith more focused. And the other foot in the world, supported by the Church, to announce Jesus's message.

He seeks God

It seems today that people repel God. Often it's simply because they don't know who

Jesus is. And the human tendency to not know something about someone prevents them from knowing him.

This can go as far as blocking in fear if the information is negative and unfair. We come to fear the one we don't know. This may be detrimental to the knowledge so necessary to enter into a relationship with God.

One day, someone who calls himself an atheist wrote on the internet: "I am an atheist, but I would like to know what you know to believe." Make no mistake, the majority of people who say they don't believe have not found reasons to believe, reasons to say that it is worth the joy of believing.

They must, however, start somewhere. They should not wait for others to convert for them, but place their trust in God. God will surprise them when the time comes, accordingly to their openness and perseverance.

At the same time, there are others who think they know who Jesus is, but who have wrong information or have misunderstood him. They will regrettably repel Jesus, because they have come to a false idea, a false image of him. If they repel Jesus, there's lacking in their lives. Without being aware of it, their heart searches for him.

Reciting the Rosary with Mary is an indispensable tool for conversion.

Let's stay sober

Peter commits us on the path that leads into the Heart of Jesus Christ. He says it in such a simple way that it could pass by without us noticing it:

"Gird up the loins of your mind, live soberly, and set your hopes completely on the grace to be brought to you at the revelation of Jesus Christ." *1 Peter, chapter 1, verse 13*

He simply says to prepare ourselves to receive Jesus when he reveals himself to us. This is our deep belief.

Let's prepare our spirit for action. To start, we need to prepare ourselves for our life to change. Then he asks us to stay "sober".

The sobriety in all things allows us to adjust our impulses and counter the exaggerations over achievements and rejoicing. With each victory for the faith, let's remain sober.

For that, let's get to know each other, learn to be aware of who we are, be a close observer of what surrounds us and know how to distinguish between good and bad.

Peter adds: "set your hopes completely on the grace to be brought to you at the revelation of Jesus Christ". Grace is received when we receive Jesus in our life.

Jesus reveals himself to us, but to receive him we need to adjust our life to his. This is our first mission. When we were young, we adjusted to what our parents taught us, said and did. But since we have entered a movement of faith, we are now adjusting to the will of Christ.

If we become disappointed later, it's because we do not put our efforts in the right places. Let's bring our boat back on course and place our compass in the direction of Jesus.

Jesus tells us:

"Many that are first will be last, and (the) last will be first." *Mark, chapter 10, verse 31*

In God, with the desire to adjust to his Sacred Heart, there will be neither last nor first. We will all be one, united in the Kingdom of God in the same eternal feast, the same worship, the same praise. Let's begin now to gather what God offers us and receive in fullness the graces to which we are entitled.

We do not live the life of Paul or Peter, or others, but we have our lives and where we are, become passers of the faith. We are here to encourage people to discover values, truth and also encourage life. Every little good intention that we deploy helps the people around us.

To share

It's important to share the Love we receive from God, so that he transforms the people around us. James gives us a major point:

"What good is it, my brothers, if someone says he has faith but does not have works?"
James, chapter 2, verse 14

God doesn't stop wanting to keep us united to him. He has put all his Love in our heart, and he wants to find this Love by a free and responsible act on our part. If not, the Love that he's placed in us, we will not recognize.

So, yes, faith, but works are also important because they are related to the neighbour and to our expression of Love for others. It must show. Otherwise, it will not show.

The works keep us moving in faith. The Love received from God and the quantity and quality we will share with others is what we receive from God. More personally, the Love we receive from God and the quantity and quality we share with others is the depth of Love we have in God.

Jesus calls the crowd with his disciples and he says to them:

> Whoever wishes to come after me must deny himself, take up his cross, and follow me. For whoever wishes to save his life will lose it, but whoever loses his life for my sake and that of the gospel will save it. *Mark, chapter 8, verses 34 to 35*

To lose a fruitless part of our life and to go against the Love of God is what should motivate us. Let's gradually lose all temptations to grief, distress and discouragement. The more we lose them, the more we will find ways to live the Love of God and offer it.

Harvest

Jesus says:

"The harvest is abundant but the labourers are few; so ask the master of the harvest to send out labourers for his harvest." *Matthew, chapter 9, verses 37 to 38*

We know this prayer. The harvest will always be abundant and the workers be few. There's no need to wait for the workers. He addresses himself to us, it's up to us to engage in it.

We can waste a lot of time looking for workers, if we seek them ourselves, because Jesus asks us to pray the harvest master for that. Let's engage and the Lord will seek them.

By asking the master to send us workers, they will introduce themselves. The time that seems lost by prayer will be regained, since it is Jesus, the master of the harvest, who will send the workers. But let's not wait, because they can work in another field. We are in ours.

May we also pray for "us" to become workers who can serve as true disciples. Let's improve our capacity to be true workers in the midst of the abundant harvest (mission) in which God sends us.

Sometimes we go from a Church of reapers to a church of sowers. When we sow, the Holy Spirit is with us. Let's also become sowers of the presence and will of God for the world.

It's easy to be among the world, but it's not always easy to detect people who are ready to walk in faith. To discover faith in the hearts of others and to reveal it to them, we must pray for them.

We also ask Jesus that faith and discernment increase. We must ask Jesus to work with us to fully perceive faith in others and to know how to gently reveal to them what they hold of the beauties, the graces received in them. To harvest, let's always look for the beauties of faith in people.

May the Holy Spirit sharpen our spiritual eye as the eagle's piercing gaze, so that we may enter from a pure and sincere heart, as sowers of the faith and workers in the harvest, and thus reveal the Love of God in hearts.

As we sow in the field of God, our spiritual life will leap to an intensity never experienced, because we will discover the wonders of the Lord in the heart of each person who decides to follow him.

Let's pray God to send workers to sow and harvest. May there be vocations that arise from all the good intentions deployed.

To speak out

Pathway 73

To claim from our mouth

Paul understands the need to evangelize:

"If you confess with your mouth that Jesus is Lord and believe in your heart that God raised him from the dead, you will be saved." *Romans, chapter 10, verse 9*

We are called to make Jesus known to humanity by beginning near us, in our circle of friends, in our family, here, where we are. Finding only one person who demonstrates a little faith and the blessing of God will unfold more.

Let's be more careful and patient with our personal family. Let's draw closer to those who show signs of faith. Others will probably follow one day. Let's leave some time for these.

We need to receive today the teaching of the Apostles, from our bishops and the Pope, to continue the mission of bringing Jesus to the world.

Andrew knew how to bring his brother to conversion and follow Jesus. Andrew had to be convincing for Simon-Peter to embark on a new "boat" named after Jesus.

Andrew says to his brother:

"We have found the Messiah." *John, chapter 1, verse 41*

And Jesus says to them,

"Come after me, and I will make you fishers of men." *Matthew, chapter 4, verse 19*

Jesus knows his position, he is God and he is in front. He invites the first Apostles to follow him, "Come after me". Let's not try to take Jesus's position. The Apostles followed him and they learned at his school for a few years. They learned the essentials of the mission that would also become theirs.

The Apostles became the leaders of a church that belongs in everything to Jesus. They didn't change the modalities of the Church, but they welcomed it from Jesus's hands, still fragile humanly, but strong because Christ is the Master. Jesus is still guiding her today. The whole Church is still following Jesus.

Paul, proud?

In the book of Sirach, it is written:

"He is a God of justice, who knows no favorites." *Sirach, chapter 35, verse 12*

God Loves all people without distinction. Whether people give themselves first or last place, that don't change God's reality. But this should be worrying for people.

Jesus places us before the scene of a pharisee who places himself first and a publican who offers himself the last place.

There's a reflection that we can realize at the outset, that of the publican or the last place. Let's start with him.

Jesus describes the scene as follows:

"The tax collector stood off at a distance and would not even raise his eyes to heaven but beat his breast and prayed, 'O God, be merciful to me a sinner.'" *Luke, chapter 18, verse 13*

He recognizes that he's a sinner and that this is the message that Jesus wants to convey to us.

But imagine that he says rather in his heart: "If I'm always in the last place, it's sure that I will become a saint and that I will enter heaven at the end of my many days." And by dint of saying, "My God, show yourself favourable to the sinner that I am," it could show that he no longer believes that the Lord is in favour. This attitude would be pride.

If he hits his chest all the time and as soon as he comes out of the Church, he does nothing but hit himself and he doesn't go to other people, we also understand that he's away from God because of the image he gives himself.

It's as if we would say to ourselves: "I will always stand in the back, because I look at myself and humble myself before the Lord."

We may want to be last, but we must be careful not to bury our talents, otherwise we fall into fear and distance from God. We are sinners, we only have to recognize it and continue to improve with Jesus.

A chance that Jesus describes the publican to us differently. He has a good attitude. He recognizes himself as a sinner and he places his trust in God. According to Jesus, he doesn't show himself superior to others.

The pharisee, for his part, takes the first place and he doesn't recognize his wrongs.

Moreover, for him, the others are wrong. "I'm not like the rest of humanity," he says:

"O God, I thank you that I am not like the rest of humanity - greedy, dishonest, adulterous - or even like this tax collector. I fast twice a week, and I pay tithes on my whole income." *Luke, chapter 18, verses 11 to 12*

Pride plucks the pharisee. He sees the faults of others and he complains about them. One is like this, the other is like that, and it goes on. He's not like the others, him.

Paul seems to have pride like the pharisee:

> I have competed well; I have finished the race; I have kept the faith. From now on the crown of righteousness awaits me, which the Lord, the just judge, will award to me on that day, and not only to me, but to all who have longed for his appearance. *2 Timothy, chapter 4, verses 7 to 8*

How to discern now between Paul who believes to have succeeded in the race and that the Lord will consider him like an Apostle of choice and the pharisee who also gives himself a first place? Then, Sirach who explicitly says that the Lord makes no difference between humans? It's interesting.

Paul, like the pharisee, gives himself the first place, the publican allows himself the last place and Sirach recalls that God makes no difference between people.

With a quick glance we could deduce that Paul is no better than the pharisee. He goes so far as to say that he deserves: "the crown of righteousness". And to add to it, it's absolutely certain that Jesus: "the Lord, the just judge, will award to me on that day".

There's a detail here that doesn't appear when we observe Paul; it's his relationship to Jesus. This is very different from the attitude of the pharisee. Paul lives an open, intimate relationship, a special relationship with

Jesus. It must be said that Paul has overcome obstacles to come to such faith.

Paul's heart changed because he opened himself to Christ and he let himself be transformed by his Light. He left the Holy Spirit a place in his life, so much so that he also lived it through by the different charisms and gifts transmitted to the community of believers. Paul is so close to Jesus that he can share his trust with others. And he adds on his testimony:

"Not only to me, but to all who have longed for his appearance."

Paul will receive the crown of righteousness as those who desire Christ with love, who advances in peace and trust in God.

Paul gives back to the community what he receives from the Holy Spirit. Paul is near Jesus. Because of Jesus, Paul can speak as he does. This is the discernment to realize with his words. He recognizes that it is God and his graces that act in his life. It's because of Jesus!

Let's receive this word from Paul:

"The Lord be with your spirit. Grace be with all of you." *2 Timothy, chapter 4, verses 22*

Then, as we go back, we return to the passage in Sirach: "He is a God of justice, who knows no favorites."

The Lord judges not, since he doesn't make differences between people.

Sirach reminds us to make our own judgment on our heart. But do we really know our heart, then the heart of the person and his real connection with Jesus? Do we go beyond the first idea we have of a person? Do we ourselves have a real experience with Jesus?

The testimony of God

Jesus said to Nicodemus and to us at the same time:

"But the one who comes from heaven (is above all). He testifies to what he has seen and heard, but no one accepts his testimony." *John, chapter 3, verses 31c to 32*

Nicodemus took a step toward Jesus and Jesus touched him. But Jesus also invites him to understand that many others don't seem to receive his testimony. This is why John writes: "no one accepts his testimony".

Peter reminds us to receive the testimony of God:

"We are witnesses of these things, as is the holy Spirit." *Acts, chapter 5, verse 32*

We become witnesses of Jesus Christ with the grace of the Holy Spirit. Let's ask the Holy Spirit to fill our lives, so that we may remain in Jesus's light. May his light keep us on the path of truth, the path of life.

Ah! If my people listened to me

There are different ways to recognize God. We will never know how important it is to listen to God's calls in our hearts and in the hearts of those around us. He wants us to receive his Love. But he's waiting for our answer. There are ways of discovering it in a gesture, a word, a feeling, an interiority. Hosea has found a way to recognize him:

"You are our God, for in you the orphan finds compassion." *Hosea, chapter 14, verse 4*

To have compassion for the orphan is a way of recognizing the presence of God. We're all orphans of Love, keeping away from God.

The Psalm contains as a sigh of God:

"If my people would listen, if Israel would walk in my paths." *Psalm 81, verse 14*

Ah, if everyone could put God first! Ah, if everyone knew how much God Loves! God Loves us as he Loves the orphan!

Here is the Lord's answer to whoever looks for him:

> I will heal their defection, I will love them freely; for my wrath is turned away from them. I will be like the dew for Israel: he shall blossom like the lily; He shall strike root like the Lebanon cedar, and put forth his shoots. His splendour shall be like the olive tree and his fragrance like the Lebanon cedar. Again they shall dwell in his shade and raise grain; they shall blossom like the vine, and his fame shall be like the wine of Lebanon. *Hosea, chapter 14, verses 5 to 8*

Beautiful! But God doesn't really have anger. It's just frustrating not being able to reach the person's heart. But also, God isn't frustrated. He waits patiently for us to open the space of our heart. God is the very patient, since he lets us free.

Jesus, in the next passage, reminds us that to love God and let ourselves be Loved by him, we must also love our neighbour and let ourselves be Love by him to the extent of what we can offer as Love received from the Lord. Jesus tells us to love God:

"With all your heart, with all your understanding, with all your strength, and to love your neighbour as yourself' is worth more than all burnt offerings and sacrifices." *Mark, chapter 12, verse 33*

This is the basis of a journey of life, an impulse of one's person in the will of God, a wish for each heart to find pure, true, real Love.

May we recognize how fortunate we are to know that the Father Loves us with infinite Love, that he has given us his Son for our salvation, and the Holy Spirit to guide us on his way.

God is launching this powerful sentence that brings us back to basics:

"It is love that I desire, not sacrifice, and knowledge of God rather than holocausts.
Hosea, chapter 6, verse 6

"It is love that I desire, not sacrifice."

We sometimes have a strange way of thinking. We think that through hard work, by forcing ourselves, we get everything we want for our spiritual life.

But faithfulness is above all what God seeks from us. It is through union with God that we will keep faith. It's certain that it takes a little effort, especially the effort to keep our life in the path that leads constantly to God. It's the importance of being attentive to the movement of the Holy Spirit in our heart.

To live an encounter, to know God and to remain faithful to this encounter from day to day, here is a route well planned. It's the only itinerary of the heart and soul of the person who wishes to live forever. To be united to God is the assurance that we will help others to join him.

Offer Baptism

The time of the Holy Spirit is the time of the founding of the Church. And this time continues today:

"When the apostles in Jerusalem heard that Samaria had accepted the word of God, they sent them Peter and John." *Acts, chapter 8, verse 14*

The Apostles note that Samaria begins to be evangelized. And they send Peter and John to strengthen the Samaritans in their faith.

As it is written:

"They prayed for them, that they might receive the Holy Spirit, for it had not yet fallen upon any of them; they had only been baptized in the name of the Lord Jesus." *Acts, chapter 8, verses 15 to 16*

What Peter and John do is to pray for the Samaritans. Here's what we should do each day, pray for the people around us. If their hearts open, Jesus will join them. Let's continue our journey and pray. Praying leads to Baptism, Baptism leads to receiving the Holy Spirit.

We can accomplish so much by prayer. Prayer breaks the walls, touches the heart, transforms lives. Prayer leads people to Jesus who leads them to the Father's house right away.

We can pray for people who come to funerals, for example. We can pray for people when we wait at the hospital, when we're in a city council, country or other. We can pray for people in a hobby or on vacation.

We don't lack works to realize when we understand that we can do so much, that we can bring people to Jesus, by the heart, by prayer. Let's sow faith by prayer. We can be right now in the house of the Father with Jesus:

"Peter and John laid hands on them and they received the holy Spirit." *Acts, chapter 8, verse 17*

They impose their hands, they place their hands on the Samaritans and they pray to the Lord for them.

This gesture is very simple and it joins the heart of the person. They also ask the Holy Spirit about these people. Peter and John received the Holy Spirit and they entered the construction of the Church, they entered into communion with the christians and with Jesus. They retransmit it.

Then, these people will be invited to be baptized. To be baptized means to enter into the life of God's Love. It's opening a door to be Loved by God. It's to accept that God Loves us. It is offering our life to God.

God already Loves us whether we are baptized or not. But he still wants us to ask him for baptism. It's a sign of our willingness to join and to receive everything from him.

Wanting Baptism for a child is an act of parental love. They want their child to enter the great family of God and to be inspired by the values that christians share.

Jesus had told us before going to the Father:

"I will ask the Father, and he will give you another Advocate to be with you always, the Spirit of truth." *John, chapter 14, verses 16 to 17*

Jesus invites us to receive the Holy Spirit. And when we receive it, he adds:

> I will ask the Father, and he will give you another Advocate to be with you always, the Spirit of truth, which the world cannot accept, because it neither sees nor knows it. But you know it, because it remains with you, and will be in you. *John, chapter 14, verses 16 to 17*

As mentioned in the Gospel of John, if the people around us don't receive Baptism and the Holy Spirit, they don't know Jesus. They are Loved by God like everyone else, but they have not necessarily chosen him.

What difference does it make in our lives when we accept the Holy Spirit and Baptism? For the regulars, they may no longer realize the presence of the Spirit in them, but he's there and he seeks to be recognized, again. Jesus likes us to seek him, to find him, to seek him again …

For those who have received Baptism, Jesus tells us:

"You know it, because it remains with you, and will be in you." *John, chapter 14, verse 17*

It is a relationship that becomes intimate with God.

Does that make us better than others? No. And yes. We're not better by our merits alone … without God. We become better because we know that God is Love. We have discovered the source of Love that we receive for free. We are invited to abide in his Love:

"I will not leave you orphans; I will come to you." *John, chapter 14, verse 18*

Jesus doesn't leave us orphans, he leaves us his Spirit who guides us to Baptism and unites us to him. Let's stay in his Love.

May the Lord turn our poverty into wealth:

"A clean heart create for me, God; renew in me a steadfast spirit. Do not drive me from your presence, nor take from me your holy spirit." *Psalm 51, verses 12 to 13*

For starters, God can't chase us away from his face. Then he never takes away the Holy Spirit. He's always present with us. On the other hand, when we rub shoulders with evil, we chase ourselves from the face and Spirit of God.

This prayer of the psalm helps us to refocus on God: "A clean heart create for me, God; renew in me a steadfast spirit." We ask God to transform our poverty by cleansing our heart and making it pure, and then we ask him to fill our spirit with his presence. Come help us Lord:

"Restore my joy in your salvation; sustain in me a willing spirit." *Psalm 51, verse 14*

Then we want for others what we ask for us:

"I will teach the wicked your ways, that sinners may return to you. (...) Lord, open my lips; my mouth will proclaim your praise." *Psalm 51, verses 15 and 17*

"That sinners", that is to say, to everyone, even to us who walk, we want to teach and learn ourselves the way of peace, joy and love. We wish that, like us, "that sinners may return to you". Our poverty will then change into wealth. We want to constantly come back to the Lord.

Lord, with a heart purified by your presence, place your words on our lips and let our mouth announce your praise. Announcing is also allowing your presence to pass through us to reach hearts:

"Instead, there shall always be rejoicing and happiness in what I create; For I create Jerusalem to be a joy and its people to be a delight." *Isaiah, chapter 65, verse 18*

God continually intends to lead us in his Love. He wants us in peace, joy, hope. Throughout the Bible, he seeks to comfort the people, he seeks to appease him. May the "people become joy". This is the way to recognize the presence of the Trinity in our heart.

May we become joy. May we observe joy in others. Complete joy is lived in God. Let's be attentive to all that God has created and in which we live and to all that God is constantly creating in us.

Rest

While on Jesus's mission, rest is important for understanding what we're learning. Jesus leads the Apostles away because they've come to live the bases for evangelization and they want to share with him what they are living. Then Jesus says to them,

"Come away by yourselves to a deserted place and rest a while." *Mark, chapter 6, verse 31*

Let's go with Jesus. May he prepare our hearts for the mission of evangelizing. Let's share all that we discover in faith and thank him for his presence in us. Let's also share with the Father and the Spirit our desire to unite to the Trinity.

Jesus is the masterpiece before our eyes. Let's rest, gather and pray, with Mary and all the saints together!

Bibliography

Bible: The new american bible, Website, *http://www.vatican.va/archive/ENG0839/_I NDEX.HTM*

Catechism of the Catholic Church, Website, *http://www.vatican.va/archive/ENG0015/_I NDEX.HTM*

Vatican Council II. Ad Gentes. The dogmatic constitution on the missionary activity of the Church, number 8,

http://www.vatican.va/archive/hist_council s/ii_vatican_council/documents/vat-ii_decree_19651207_ad-gentes_en.html

Table of contents